Selling: The No-Nonsense Guide

Selling
The No-Nonsense Guide

James Farrell

BLACKHALL
PUBLISHING

Published by
Blackhall Publishing
Lonsdale House
Avoca Avenue
Blackrock
Co. Dublin
Ireland

e-mail: info@blackhallpublishing.com
www.blackhallpublishing.com

ISBN: 978-1-84218-184-3

A catalogue record for this book is available from the British Library.

Printed in Ireland by ColourBooks Ltd.

For my daughters, Emma, Rachel and Abbi

Preface

In 1974 on the 15th of December the country was on the annual feel good trip – Christmas. The lights were on, the trees were up and the sparkle was out. Unfortunately I was at a funeral. My mother had died. I was seventeen. It wasn't good, my poor Mam was dead and the old man found it difficult to cope. Family life was a little chaotic and to be perfectly honest, in the economically depressed 70s, life appeared a little grim and the future a little hopeless, or so it appeared to me.

I was at that stupid age, looking for something and easily led. I could see young lads like myself turning to drink and drugs. All the temptations and influences were there and they did look appealing and even cool. And I played that game; it can easily become a lifestyle when there is little else on your horizon.

So what has this to do with sales and a book on selling skills? Let me explain. At that time I got a part-time job as a door-to-door salesperson selling aluminium windows. Not exactly a glamorous start to a career in business but in my case it was a lifesaver. I began to realise that you can have control over what happens to you. You could influence outcomes. In this case the more doors I knocked on the more sales I could make. I could determine my own future, my own success; it was in my hands. Sales and selling was a liberating force and it would sustain me all my life through good times and bad.

Now I'm not proposing a selling career as a therapy for insecure adolescences who find themselves in difficult circumstances, but it worked for me and I am grateful for that.

Not long after I left school I got a job as a wages clerk in Dublin Port. I worked in the office of Dublin Port Stevedores and our job was to calculate the wages for the dockers in the port. The most challenging part of the work was explaining to dockers how you had arrived at a figure that was at odds with their own expectations. Explaining tax free allowances and tax bands in such circumstances was at times bizarre and sometimes a little scary.

Shortly afterwards I won a scholarship to study Marketing in Dublin Institute of Technology and off I went. After four years I emerged with a degree. I thought I'd find myself a career job in one of the few major companies operating in Ireland in the depressed late 1970s and early 1980s. What I soon realised was that the national symbol for Ireland was a harp, and it was for a reason – you had to pull strings to get anywhere. Without any connections and an ordinary background I had no chance of finding my first steps on the corporate ladder.

Over the following years I worked in selling jobs of one kind or another. Very often they were commission only, door-to-door sales. There were others that involved selling to retailers and others still that required selling to businesses. There was a common theme: all my jobs involved finding new customers and generating leads. The commission was the dominant focus and I'm afraid I never had a job that provided sales leads. It was not long before I went into business for myself. When I say business for myself it sounds as if it was something substantial and established. Believe me, that was far from the truth. I did all sorts. One of my first ventures was making and selling button badges. They were all the rage and I bought a machine in England which I duly smuggled through the north of Ireland, thus avoiding the customs duties and the custom officers who were stationed along the border. I made badges and sold them to music record shops across the country. In time I included T-shirts and various other pop paraphernalia. Over the years I did a little more smuggling, which was a precarious business along the border at the height of the Troubles.

However, not long afterwards I went on to sell more conventional products and use more mainstream methods of importing. I continued to work for myself, primarily in direct sales. I have sold key-cutting machines, cash registers, office equipment, quality management systems and a lot more, which we'll talk about as we go along. I have sold at the highest levels, including presentations to boards of directors of global organisations. I have seen a fair number of highs and plenty of lows.

I have often supplemented my income through teaching. It was teaching that led me into my present business, corporate training. Today I am the founder and managing director of Professional Development Ltd, Ireland's biggest private training provider with a sales turnover in the millions. We sell and market training courses in over forty different topics, including sales, management, customer service and many more. We operate in Dublin, Cork, Galway, Limerick and Belfast. We also have a base in the UK offering courses in Manchester and London.

Contents

Preface		**vii**
Introduction		**1**
1.	**Selling Is Simple**	**3**
	What Is Selling?	4
2.	**You Can Do It**	**7**
	Confidence	7
	Good Talker	8
	How You Look	9
3.	**What You'll Need to Succeed**	**11**
	Product Knowledge	11
	Selling Skills	13
	Attitude – How to Get Your Head Right	14
	Attitude, Not Ability	14
	Danger of Negativity	15
	How You See Things	16
4.	**The Myth of the Motivational Talk**	**19**
	Nurturing Your Obsession	20
	How to Set Goals	20
	Tips for Goal Setting	22
5.	**Where Does the Sale Start?**	**23**
	You Are How You Look	24
	Don't Be Too Obvious	25
	The Talking Bit	25
	Advantages of a Planned Pitch	27
6.	**How to Make a Sales Pitch**	**29**
	Stages of the Sale	30

Contents

	Sales Presentations Are Conversations	30
	You Must Control the Conversation	30
7.	**Finding Out What Your Customer Wants**	**33**
	Understanding Your Customer	33
	Why Customers Buy Your Product	35
	Take Your Time, Understand Your Customer	36
	No One Ever Talked You into Anything	37
	When I Thought About It, I Changed my Mind	39
	Telling Is Not Selling	39
	God Forbid	40
8.	**Getting Customers to Convince Themselves**	**41**
	Volvo, the Safe Car	41
	So Let's Recap	43
9.	**How to Get Customers Talking**	**45**
	How to Communicate	45
	Open and Closed Questions	46
	Questions at the Heart of Selling	48
	Concentrate on Your Customer	48
	How to Influence Your Customer's Feelings Towards You	50
	Wait Until You Get It All, Don't Rush	51
	Sample Questions for You to Use	52
	Are You the Right Man?	55
	What's the Budget?	56
10.	**How to Start the Selling Conversation**	**57**
	Opening the Sale	57
	The Barney School of Sales Training	57
	Building Rapport with Customers	59
	Your Opening Lines	61
	Changing the Expectation from Being Told to Being Asked	62
11.	**Presenting Your Product**	**67**
	Knowing What People Buy	67

Contents

	Product Features, Only Half the Story	68
	Making the Link	69
	As Big As Your Imagination	70
	It's About the Customer, Not You	71
	Make It Crystal Clear	73
	It Doesn't Come Naturally	74
12.	**Turning Around Stalls and Objections**	**75**
	What Do You Think?	76
	Why Sellers Don't Handle Resistance	80
	A Technique for Dealing with Objections	83
	People Don't Always Tell the Truth	86
	Dealing with Hidden Concerns	87
	You Bring It Up	88
13.	**Getting Your Price**	**91**
	Buyers Don't Always Buy on Price	93
	Here Is Another Thing We Know About Price	93
	The Real Cost of Giving a Discount	94
	Price Cutting Is Often Unnecessary	97
	How to Deal with Price Challenges	98
	Sell Your Price, Sell the Difference	99
	Put the Difference in Perspective	100
	What Extra for the Extra Cost?	100
	Discounting	101
14.	**Sealing the Deal, Closing the Sale**	**103**
	Not How, But When	104
	Just One More Thing	105
15.	**Finding New Customers Without Cold Calling**	**107**
	Show Me the Buyers	108
	How to Find Customers	110
	The Warm Knock Rather than the Cold Call	110
	The Warm Knock	111
	The System for Warm Knocking	113
	Don't Worry, You're Normal	115

	Know Your Numbers	116
	A Workshop	117
16.	**Sales Management**	**121**
	Managers	122
	Pretensions	124
	How It Goes Wrong	125
	Another Way	125
	Sales Measures	126
	Don't Judge Salespeople on Sales	127
	Standards of Performance	128
	Conclusion	**131**
	Planned Sales Presentation	**133**

Introduction

When I started in the training business in the late 1980s the only course of any interest to the business community was sales training. Sales was the big thing and for a very good reason. At the time, with the economy in the doldrums, the main challenge was business development. With money tight and prospects few, most people in business were acutely aware of the necessity of honing their selling skills. A memory from one of my first selling jobs may give you an idea.

I had taken a job selling key-cutting machines and my boss was explaining the workings of the machines. When he had described the operations of the machine he said, 'There's just one other thing, never forget the nutritional value of these machines.' I looked at him completely puzzled before he went on, 'If you don't sell them, you won't eat.'

If you could sell in that highly competitive market you would make a living – you wouldn't get rich but you would get by. Roll on the years and we developed into a booming economy and with a modicum of selling ability you could make a fortune. You would imagine that the acquisition of selling skills would be a priority, but you'd be wrong.

In fact when I was approached to write this book I was sceptical as I didn't believe there was an appetite for selling skills. It would appear that in buoyant and developed economies people prefer to develop other loftier skills. Emotional intelligence, mind mapping and neuro-linguistic programming are the order of the day.

Don't get me wrong, I'm not a Luddite when it comes to new ideas and innovations but if you have been in this business as long as I have, you too would be a little cynical. Every other year there is a new theory or innovation. If it's not quality circles it's re-engineering. This stuff is like diets, there is a new one every year. I'm sure these innovative ideas offer real benefits and have validity. However I do know with absolute certainty the ability to sell, persuade and influence others is a critical business skill and should be the starting point for anyone with aspirations to succeed in business.

In boom times you'll survive in business without an eye to sales. But, in time, booming markets turn, as they always do. Then of course it will be back to basics and the ability to sell and make sales will be a priority.

In Ireland we have done well, very well. But now Eastern European and emerging economies across the world present a challenge. The differences between us and them are marginal. Our ability to amplify our minor differences and advantages is what are described as selling skills. Our capacity to continue to thrive is dependent, I believe, on our acquisition of those skills – hence this book.

1

Selling Is Simple

For starters I don't know everything. Some people who write books, and particularly those who write selling books, pretend they know it all. They have an answer for everything; no matter what is said to them they can respond with that perfect reply.

Well not me, but I do know a little about sales. I know it's not black magic or being smarter than everyone else. It's simple common sense and if you thought about it for any period of time, you too would realise that it's simple and logical.

When you finish this book you'll probably conclude 'that was basic', and you'd be right. You see, selling has been shrouded in myth. All sorts of nonsense have been written and spoken, especially by those who present themselves as sales gurus or experts. There are many who spend a lot of time making simple things complex. Through a mixture of pop psychology and the application of complex models to what are simple processes they come up with some bizarre conclusions, and no more so than in the area of sales.

My own particular favourite is the one where you're told to 'focus on the tip of the person's nose when you are speaking to them'. This, we are told, will give the impression that you, as a salesperson, are interested and attentive.

I don't know about you, but for me, one of two things will happen. Either you'll get a headache or you'll get dizzy as your eyes dart from nose tip to eyes, which is the natural place to look when you're speaking to someone.

I think it's safe to conclude that selling is simpler than you'd think and definitely easier and less complicated than the so-called experts would have you believe. It is something that can be learned, without a lot of effort, and it can be learned by anyone.

I also think that selling is a skill we all need. As someone said somewhere, 'Everyone lives by selling something'. Whether you are a politician, poet or priest you're selling. You are selling a message; you are seeking to influence, to persuade, to have others see things as you see them. Selling is not the sole remit of the businessperson but a life skill, required by all.

So there you have it, selling is simple and a necessary life skill. So what is this thing called selling?

What Is Selling?

Probably the best way to describe selling is to tell you what it is not. I know I said this thing was simple, but bear with me for a minute.

Selling is not fast talking. Despite the stereotypical image of a salesperson as someone who has the gift of the gab – someone who has not only kissed the Blarney Stone but bit it – that is not selling. Selling is not tricks. It is not smart answers and it definitely is not forcing people to buy.

In fact we couldn't force people to buy even if we wanted to but, surprisingly, we don't want to. By putting pressure on people you may occasionally win a sale but you won't win customers. And it is customers and repeat customers who build businesses. No, the hard sell doesn't work.

We have all had the experience of walking into a shop and being pounced on by that over-eager salesperson. A hasty retreat is your normal reaction. This is hardly the way to make sales and build business. The hard sell doesn't work on you, and it won't work for you. The obvious sell doesn't work either. The salesperson with the too-firm handshake and the Miss World smile will be seen for what they are. An obvious salesperson isn't a good salesperson.

Good selling is not about being too pushy but neither is it about being too nice. Most people are concerned about being pushy, but, in reality, if we have a failing, it is that we are not pushy enough. It is not a case of too much, but not enough.

The real problem is that we are all too nice. Lots of people employed as sellers wear smart suits, drive around the country in nice cars and call on people and have pleasant chats. That's not selling, that's tourism. As we will see, selling is little more sophisticated than that.

So if that is what selling is not, let me describe what selling is. Selling is making it easy for people to agree with you. Selling is making it easy for people to buy. The easier you make it for people to buy the more they will buy. And there are examples all around us. Let me give you just one. When I was a young fella, shops had doors; you pushed the door, the bell rang and you were in the shop. Once in the shop you approached the counter and behind the counter was all the merchandise. Sound familiar? Well it was, but no more. Today retailers don't have restrictive doors, they don't have counters, in fact there are few or no barriers between you and the merchandise. Yes, they have cash desks but no barriers. They have made it easier for you to buy and the easier it is, the more you buy – simple.

Face-to-face selling is just the same, we present and describe products in such away that it is easy for buyers to see the benefits. The skills and techniques to make it easy for people to buy are what is known as selling.

It needs to be learned and practised. It requires you to have a structured approach to dealing with potential buyers and that is the theme of this book. You will discover that good sellers don't do anything radically different, just slightly different. You will learn to talk to buyers in a manner that allows them to see clearly the benefits of your product or service. It is subtle, gentle and non-intrusive. It is the art of selling.

2

You Can Do It

When we think of sellers we form a picture in our mind. We think of someone who is dapper, articulate and confident, with a good line in chat. That might be the picture but it isn't the true story, not by a long shot. In fact many of us rule ourselves out because we don't see ourselves as outgoing enough. We're not confident enough, we just haven't got the patter. These might be commonly held views, but common or not they are just plain untrue.

Actually it amazes me just how persuasive people are in telling you they are not the selling type. Yes, they will absolutely convince you, and of course themselves, that selling is not for them. They will completely sell you on the idea that they can't sell.

Let me clarify a few basic facts from the outset.

Confidence

Who among us can say that they are truly confident? Very few I would imagine and those who do proclaim to be absolutely confident are normally drunk or mad. Let me tell you a true story to illustrate.

A number of years ago I was speaking at a conference in Dublin and I began by saying that we could all do with a little more confidence. I asked for a show of hands for those who agreed with me and sure enough every one of the couple of hundred people put up their hand up, with the exception of one guy in the second row. He was sitting with a number of young people who I assumed to be his staff. This genius was not prepared to admit any shortcomings – a bit of a David Brent from *The Office*. Anyway, maybe it was a little unkind of me but I couldn't resist: I invited him to address the audience as to the source of his great assuredness. As to his response, well the word 'nappy' should aptly define the moment.

Of course confidence is important but don't let your lack of it rule you out. Sufficient confidence can be acquired and as we progress I'll explain how you can develop it. And it's not psychology, it is simple preparation. If you know exactly what you are going to say and how you're going to say it you'll have the confidence. It's a bit like the fellow who can't string a sentence together without stuttering and yet when he's asked to sing he'd put Ol' Blue Eyes to shame he is so word perfect. Why? Because he knows the exact words and as a result he's confident. And so will you be if you do the preparation.

Good Talker

This is probably the biggest misconception of them all. We have this vision of a salesperson as someone who is so glib that they could talk you into anything. Well the fast talker may delay you or bore you, but they won't convince you. You see, selling is not about talking, it is about conversations; conversations that you control and guide but you don't dominate.

So a seller is a good conversationalist rather than a big talker. So what's a good conversationalist? Let's suppose you go out with a friend for an evening. Your friend invites you to talk about your job, with further encouragement you proceed onto your family and just when you are getting onto your views on the current offerings on the TV soaps the barman calls time. Not a bad evening, very enjoyable and what a good conversation with a great conversationalist.

If you reflect on the people who you enjoy most, you'll find they are the people who allow and encourage you to talk. A good conversationalist doesn't do the talking, they allow you to talk. As a simple guide, remember you have two ears and one mouth; you should use them in proportion.

Developing conversations where you encourage the customer to describe and explain is an essential part of selling. Yet over-talking by salespeople is the most common mistake. I think what happens is that we are so anxious and enthusiastic that we, as sellers, talk too much. What can happen is we sell something, and we talk so much, we end up buying it back. Unlike most other human endeavours, in selling the less you do the more you achieve.

How You Look

Sellers are generally well presented and you should be too. And as you will see first impressions are important. But be careful, while you must present yourself in a certain way the important thing is that you conform to your buyers' expectations. Here's an example.

Many years ago I was selling into music record shops and as you would expect shop managers were casual, cool people. At the time long hair and very casual dress was the norm. I as a salesperson was dressed in the usual suit and tie. As I was generally the same age as these people I decided in a fit of inspiration that I too would attire myself in a less formal outfit. It went down like a lead balloon; cool and all as the buyers were their expectation was that a supplier would be a professional business-person. Wannabe hippies just didn't fit the bill.

Now I do realise that dress codes have changed and flexibility is now the norm but the point is still valid: you must conform to your buyers' expectations. Just suppose you were to visit your doctor and when you walk into the surgery door you are met by someone who looks like a refugee from a heavy metal concert. It doesn't exactly inspire confidence.

3

What You'll Need to Succeed

To succeed in selling there are three essential ingredients. These are all you will require to prosper as a salesperson, we can all acquire them and in my opinion and experience you can do so with ease. However, they are not equally important so let's look at them in order of importance.

Product Knowledge

No matter what you are selling it is important you have an understanding and knowledge of your product, service or idea. You should also have a belief in your offering.

The type of product knowledge you will require as a seller is different to what you would need as a technician. The technician must know what goes into a product, you as a seller must know what a buyer can get out of it. Simply put, you don't have to be a mechanic to sell a car but as a car salesperson you must know what the driver can get out of the car in terms of comfort, safety, enjoyment and even status and prestige. You must know how your product compares to others and its relative competitive advantages.

I would also suggest that too much product knowledge can be a problem for sellers. Have you had the experience of buying a PC from a computer nerd? I rest my case.

So how much knowledge do you require? You need enough to feel confident in describing and discussing your product and how it can be used and enjoyed.

As for belief in your product, it is often said that 'if you don't believe in it you can't sell it'. And I suppose that's true, but it's difficult to maintain loyalty to your product, particularly when buyers continue to downplay its advantages. When you are consistently told 'ah sure they're all the same' or 'it's too expensive', such putdowns eat away at our belief in the product. That's why it is essential that we know the nature of buyers and how they behave; that too is knowledge. You, as a seller, must understand buyer behaviour, and we will deal with that as we progress.

Here is a simple tip for how much product knowledge you'll need. Marketing people spend a lot of time, money and effort in compiling product brochures and websites. They incorporate all the features, advantages, benefits and competitive offerings of the product. Here is the written testament of your product: you should study, learn and know it in detail. Very often, believe it or not, salespeople are unfamiliar with the information contained in their own product brochures and websites. Here's a challenge – take a brochure and invite a salesperson to answer questions on information contained in that brochure. You'll be surprised with the results.

Product knowledge is a perquisite for selling but in my estimation it represents just 20 per cent of what you'll need to know to succeed in sales. As you will see, the person who is the most familiar and most knowledgeable about a product is not always the most successful seller.

Selling Skills

I suppose it's obvious to say that to succeed in sales you'll need to know selling techniques. But let's be clear as to what that incorporates. There are two aspects to selling.

Sales Presentation Skills

Presentation techniques describe how you conduct sales conversations. They outline how you open the conversation, how you direct that conversation, how you best present your product or service, how you deal with hesitancy from the buyer, how and when you close the sale and finally how you reassure the buyer that they have made the right decision.

Organisational Skills

Planning and organisation are key elements in the selling process. Setting objectives and determining actions to achieve those objectives form part and parcel of the toolkit of a seller. As you will see, new business development requires disciplined and organised behaviour.

Most people would relate to the presentation aspects of selling and are surprised at the emphasis on organisational skills. It is a mistake to think that organisation is not a key selling skill. Badly organised and sloppy sellers justify their behaviour with remarks such as, 'I'm a people person; I'm not so good at detail.' What rubbish! If you have ever had to mop up after a sloppy seller you'll know what I mean. Yes, they make sales but they lose customers. They over-promise, under-deliver and generally waste time for themselves and everybody else. Be very clear, selling skills are not a menu from which you can choose the bits you like. If you can't organise yourself, you can't sell. Show me an organised, consistent and persistent seller and I'll show you a good one.

Attention to detail is almost seen as something that is for other, lesser people and not for those who work on a bigger canvas. I don't think I'm that arrogant but I've certainly not been as attentive to detail in the past as I should have been. Consistently over the years I've neglected to get this signed, or that clarified or some other omission, which all resulted in extra work needlessly.

Attitude, How to Get Your Head Right

Selling skills do work; the practices, principles and techniques of selling are tried and trusted. But they don't work for a lot of salespeople. Why? Because they lack the essential ingredients: attitude and desire. Make no mistake, no amount of product knowledge or selling technique will compensate for attitude. Yet attitude will compensate for an awful lot. Take a situation that I have seen many times: a young man joins a sales team, he's a little unsure of the product and he has limited experience or grasp of selling. Yet at every turn, he outperforms the other, more experienced, salespeople. How come this relative novice is so successful? Is it beginner's luck? No, he simply has the drive, the excitement and the attitude to succeed.

Attitude, Not Ability

Success in selling is more about attitude and desire than anything else. It is desire not ability that is the crucial factor. Consider this scenario for a moment. Just suppose I said to you I have a wonderful product I'd like you to sell. It's a decorative jewellery box that normally sells for

€280 but I can let you have it for a mere €30. How many do you think you'd sell? Not many I'd imagine. Now let's suppose I used another approach and said, if you sell 100 of them, I'll give you €25,000. Now do you think you'd sell them? Of course you would, no question. So let me ask you, what's changed? Your desire has changed. It's about desire not ability.

In the selling profession, unlike many others, you will not succeed without the correct attitude. For example, if you are a truck driver and you hate your boss and the lousy stinking company you work for, you'll probably still manage to do the journey and the job. In sales you won't, full stop.

Danger of Negativity

Attitude is an absolute necessity in selling and we must always be on our guard against negativity, which is in us and all around us. Some people are totally consumed by negativity. They can always find reasons why something can't be done and they can be very convincing. They'll tell you, 'we tried that before, it didn't work', 'the competition have it sown up', 'things are bad in the States; it's only a matter of time before it hits here', 'the pollen count is high' – any rubbish as long as it can be contrived as a reason why something won't work.

And negativity is very strong. Just imagine I told you I spoke to 100 people who know you and just one of them said they didn't like you. Who would you be interested in talking to me about? I can hear you now: 'It was that so-and-so wasn't it?' and on you'd go. The fact that 99 people thought you were a lovely person is all out-weighed by that one so-and-so. Negativity is indeed very strong.

There is an upside for negative people though. You might never make it in sales but you'll never by lonely. Go into any bar in town and say, 'I think things are on a downturn'; there will be a queue to join you in conversation. Since the start of the Celtic Tiger in Ireland there has been a whole tribe wishing and willing its demise and when the downturn came, as it always does, they felt vindicated. By the way, if you are always predicting disaster you'll one day get it right. Misery loves company.

A negative attitude is a disease that you as a seller can't afford to catch. It is a virulent virus and very contagious so be careful who you mix with. Your attitude is the key instrument in your tool box and like a carpenter you shouldn't allow anyone to blunt your chisel.

How You See Things

So how does this attitude thing work? Let me explain the simple logic of attitude. Selling and success in general is all about how you see things and how you think.

If you approach a task with the attitude that it 'can't be done' what you will do, given human nature, is to go on to find other reasons and further reasons why it is impossible to do the task. And I have no doubt that you will find many reasons to justify your 'can't be done' position. On the other hand, let's imagine you think and believe it can be done. What happens then is you become creative and innovative in your search for solutions. You let your imagination go, you problem solve, you search and dig deep.

And it still amazes me just how creative and innovative people can become. Let me give you a practical example. God forbid you were sent to prison but let's say you find yourself incarcerated. And it is suggested to you that you make an escape attempt. You now have two choices, you can think 'I can' or you can think 'I can't'. If you think you can you will become observant, creative and innovative. People have conquered what seemed like insurmountable obstacles in their escape efforts and succeeded. And what's the starting point: how you see it, how you think.

For most people the first option is to choose the easy option. I think I can't. For successful people, be it in sales or elsewhere, the magic words are 'yes I can'.

So the lesson here is whether you think you can or you think you can't, you're right. The choice is yours.

At this stage I'd like to tell you a little story. It's an old one but I think it's a good one. There was a small company in rural Ireland that manufactured shoes. As a shoe manufacturer, they of course were aware of globalisation.

Not to be outdone they decided to expand their operation. They, in their wisdom, decided to send a salesperson to the desert to sell shoes. Duly a salesperson was recruited and dispatched to the Sahara desert. Two weeks passed and they got a phone call. A dejected salesperson was on the phone: 'It's no use, nobody wears shoes here.' The luckless salesperson returned home. But companies being companies another was recruited and sent off to the desert. Two weeks passed and not a word. Another two weeks and the sales manager decided he should phone. He eventually contacted the shoe salesperson. The seller apologised for not being in touch. He explained he was too busy. He said in a hushed, but excited, voice, 'I've discovered that no one has shoes out here, I can't believe my luck!'

I hope at this stage you are now convinced of the value of having a positive outlook. But being convinced and having a positive attitude are two different things. Just because someone like me suggests that attitude is an imperative doesn't mean you will wake up in the morning with a positive attitude. It's akin to a doctor telling a clinically depressed patient to 'be happy'; it's just not that simple.

We must have a vehicle that helps us develop and maintain that attitude, day in, day out. Most of us in business have had the experience of hearing a motivational speaker and yes, we come away feeling positive and upbeat. The problem is, it lasts as long as chewing gum.

The key to acquiring a positive attitude and maintaining a focus is goal setting.

4

The Myth of the Motivational Talk

As I said in the last chapter the value of motivational speakers and the pep talk, so loved by managers, is short-lived. Yes, you might be pumped up for a day or two but in the long run you'll need more.

Goal setting and objective mapping is the kind of aspirational stuff you'd expect to see in any self-help book. And I must admit I recoil at the thought of all that almost biblical commitment to defining your goals and realising your dreams.

However goal and objective setting can be a very practical and pragmatic exercise and it can and does offer benefits. I do believe in goals.

If you think about it, the one common denominator among those people who succeed at whatever is success to them is that they have what I can only describe as an obsession. Now success can be all sorts of things to all sorts of people. To some it's sports, others business and so on. Some are born with that obsession and it is a lifelong endeavour to achieve their goal. Most people who possess an obsession will, given average ability, succeed.

I think we have all met and known someone who has had an obsession. You know the guy: you're talking to him while you are waiting at a bus stop and he tells you that he intends becoming a racing driver. You are waiting for the punchline, but it doesn't come. Just more of his insistent, excited racing car talk. How he is going to develop his career and how he has bought the book and watched the video. Jaysus, this guy is serious, God help him. He even has a girlfriend, who looks normal.

Bus arrives; the whole journey is racing car talk. Getting off that bus, you just know in your heart and soul that you have been talking to a racing car driver.

You, and for that matter he, don't know how he is going to get there, but both of you know, he'll be there.

So there you have it, the key to success is to grow yourself an obsession.

Nurturing Your Obsession

There is any amount of books written on the topic of goal setting and there are some great authorities on the subject but I'm not one of them. I believe that the essence of success is based on your ability to set and define a goal that defines success for you.

How to Set Goals

The goal-setting route, in my humble opinion, is as follows:

1. Decide your goal.
    It is very important that you are clear on what your goal is. Most people if asked will give you the usual generalities: make money, have my own business and so on. For goals to be your engine you must be very clear, very definite and very precise about what you want. And you must be true to yourself. Ask yourself what you really want.

2. See it in your mind's eye.
   Picture yourself, what will it be like when you achieve your goal. What will you drive, where will you live. See yourself as you will be. How will it look, how will you look. See yourself talking to others when it has happened. Let your imagination bring you there. See it, taste it, feel it.

   Don't be overly concerned about how you are going to get there. Just be sure that you will arrive.

3. Set milestones.
   There is a difference between dreamers and planners. Planners are people who realise that you have to set targets; you have to have stages to map your growth. So set milestones and focus on the next goal while keeping in mind your final destination.

4. Write it down.
   Ever since Moses came down from the mountain with the Ten Commandants written in stone, we have had respect for the written word. Respect your dream, write it down. Write down where you want to be and what the stages along the way are. Be very clear about what you want to achieve, you don't have to know how you are going to get there. Let me put it to you this way: a drunk always finds his way home. He knows where he is going; he just hasn't the clarity to understand how he is going to get there. But he'll get there.

   Write your goal down and refer to it on a regular basis.

Tips for Goal Setting

Don't be too realistic; most people set attainable goals. Often they are easily attainable, they are too realistic. They are limiting factors; don't be afraid to dream, and don't be afraid to stretch yourself beyond the reasonable.

Don't tell everyone; tell some but not others. Tell those people who are capable of vision, of seeing beyond the reasonable and who understand the attainable. The others, well be careful – they can steal your dream and prevent it from becoming a reality; they can drown you with pessimism.

Buy a book by some of the known authorities and follow their advice because selling depends on attitude and attitude is born of obsession and obsession is driven by your world view and your place in that world.

End of bleedin' sermon.

5

Where Does the Sale Start?

W hen the buyer says 'I'll take it' that's when the accountant starts his work, but for us in selling it begins way before that. But where does it begin? I'd like to tell you about an experiment I used at seminars some years ago. I'd invite a colleague of mine to join me on the platform. He would walk on without uttering a word and stand before the audience. I'd ask the audience to describe my friend from the list below.

HONEST	SLICK	CONFIDENT
PROFESSIONAL	INTELLIGENT	UNEASY
SLY	IMPULSIVE	AGGRESSIVE
MARRIED	EXTROVERT	EMOTIONAL
COMPETITIVE	TRUSTWORTY	NICE

As he would look at them expressionlessly, they would stare at him. After a moment, when they would have had a chance to study him, I'd ask for their views.

To a person everyone would have an opinion. Some would describe him as honest, others as sly, yet more as trustworthy and some would describe him as competitive. What was amazing, and what I found fascinating, was that everyone was able to make a judgement. Here were people who were willing to make profound decisions about another and yet that person had said or done nothing.

You Are How You Look

The reality is we judge people all the time based on appearance and first impressions. So where does the sale begin? The sale is on before you ever open your mouth. We form impressions of others within five to ten seconds of meeting them. The reason you don't catch people's names, having been introduced, is that you are too busy studying them. You haven't enough time for names; you're so focused on deciding what they are you didn't bother about who they are.

And don't underestimate the strength of these feelings. Maybe you go to the same bus stop every morning at the same time, and there is someone who also catches the same bus every morning, someone who you don't know and who you have never spoken to. And there you are: you just can't stand them. In fact you have decided you hate them. Not hate, in that you'll think about them beyond the bus journey, but enough for it to arise the next morning when you see them again.

We judge people, we judge them instantly and we are merciless. And these judgements are based on little things, details; all sorts of little details, about you and how you look. We judge people, places and even whole businesses on minor little things. As you go into a restaurant and you notice the glass door to be grubby you've already made up your mind.

Now I'm not going to bore you or insult you by telling you about your hair or nails or any of that stuff. What I will say is that at the beginning of the sale the focus is on you, not your product. And that's important, people buy people first. If they buy you, they will buy from you and if they don't they won't – if you get what I mean.

Don't Be Too Obvious

However be careful of the overkill. I've already mentioned the salesperson with the over-firm handshake, and don't tell me that's not common. Another one that is nearly always mentioned in selling books and is also a victim of overkill is 'maintain eye contact'. That explains all these salespeople going around with eyes out on stalks.

The classic example of the over-obvious and phoney is the air hostess. You know the one: you have just landed after a long-haul flight and the hostess who has been running up and down that plane for the last ten hours is now positioned at the exit. As you pass she beams with a huge smile and says, 'have a nice day'. Now you and I know she'd sooner kick you and all those other annoying passengers down those steps than see you have a nice day.

The Talking Bit

Selling of course has to do with presenting – the talking bit. Your presentation as a salesperson must be planned, and meticulously so. Now that might seem obvious to you, it's certainly plain common sense to me. Yet it is astounding how many so-called sales professionals will argue this one with you. They'll say you can't plan your presentation: 'sure all customers are different', 'you've got to play it by ear'. What utter nonsense.

All customers are different but their concerns are generally the same. They are concerned about price, quality, reliability; all the usual things. Let me be absolutely clear about this: if you are selling a product for, say, two weeks, you are unlikely to be asked any question or hear any comment you have not already heard. After two weeks there will be few surprises, very few. Therefore it is only logical that you would plan your presentation. Just suppose you where a guest on *Who Wants to Be a Millionaire?* and you knew the questions beforehand, tell me now you wouldn't plan your answers.

Remember in the selling situation you have about five minutes to make your mark. All that advertising, all that marketing, all that effort has one objective: to get you – the professional salesperson – in front of a live potential customer. Now you tell me you want to 'play it by ear'? Not bloody likely!

How many times have you had an argument with someone and afterwards were kicking yourself that you didn't say this or that? Often, I would imagine. In fact it is quite likely that you'd spend the rest of the day or indeed the week rerunning the episode in your mind. I've done it myself and when I retell the story, to anyone who will listen, I normally win the argument. That's human nature I suppose. Believe me, for salespeople who do not plan their sales presentation they too rerun the sale and in the second version they always win the sale, but of course it never appears on their sales figures at the end of the month.

It's really funny when you think of it how some salespeople think. Take a salesman who is invited to be best man at a friend's wedding. He will spend an inordinate amount of time preparing his speech. Books on speeches will be bought, hours spent in front of the mirror practising, further time boring his partner with 'listen to this bit, do you think it's funny?' And all to entertain a group of friends who have probably over-entertained themselves at the bar before the speeches even began.

Yet the same salesperson who depends on presentations to put food on the table, educate their children and put a roof over their head just can't be bothered to plan, they want to 'play it by ear'. And I'll give you a good one – those who practise the unplanned version normally end up with a consistent line of patter anyway, the only difference is theirs is ill-considered, inadequate and unplanned.

You must know your planned presentation as well as you know your prayers.

Your prayers may serve you in the next life, your presentation will provide for you in this one.

Over the next few chapters I'm going to offer you a planned and structured approach to making sales presentations. A planned and practised presentation will give the following distinct advantages.

Advantages of a Planned Pitch

Confidence Builder

As you will know exactly what you are going to say, when you are going to say it and how you are going to say it you will feel and appear more confident. Remember our stuttering friend from earlier who was invited to sing.

Feel Relaxed

As a fully prepared salesperson you feel more relaxed. You will be less anxious and as such avoid the temptation to talk too much – the graveyard for many a prospective salesperson. An anxious salesperson will not inspire confidence in a buyer and a buyer must have confidence in you; remember they are about to make a decision.

Be Attentive to Your Customer

As you will see, a key selling skill is the ability to read your potential buyer. When you are struggling to think of what to say next you have a limited opportunity to study your buyer.

All in all the often quoted saying 'he who fails to plan, plans to fail' is very true.

6

How to Make a Sales Pitch

As indicated earlier the sales presentation should follow a logical structure, yet it should not be rigid or inflexible. You may be familiar with the term 'selling script'? I'm not sure I like that term. It implies something an actor would learn to relate to another. In selling we don't have the luxury of teaching our buyers their lines. So it's not a script; it's a structure.

I'm now going to outline the content of that structure. At this stage you'll have to get involved, you'll be required to consider your product or service in the context of the structure as described. As I go through each step you should apply the ideas to your situation. Any passengers who do not want to get actively engaged should get off at the next stop.

Here's an idea for you: get a sheet of paper, maybe A4 size or, even better, A3 to give you lots of room, and as we go through the selling process complete each section as it applies to your product (see sample sheet at the end of the book). I know it sounds a bit like *Blue Peter*, but trust me. On completion you will have a planned presentation that is thought out and considered – and all on one piece of paper.

The stages we will be covering are as follows, and your sheet of paper should follow this format.

Stages of the Sale

- Opening the sales conversation
- Determining the buyer's needs
- Presenting your case
- Dealing with the buyer's concerns
- Dealing with the price
- Closing the sale
- After the sale

Sales Presentations Are Conversations

You must always remember that the sale is a conversation that you must guide and control. It is not a monologue, it is a dialogue and the buyer's participation is critical to the outcome. You should always stick to the format and avoid letting the buyer dictate. And that can very easily happen. For example, just suppose for a moment you are selling a digital camera. The buyer commences by saying, 'They are all very expensive.' If you proceed to answer this assertion and defend the cost of the cameras you have lost control.

In fact it is unfair to you and the buyer to start by discussing price. In normal circumstances an average buyer is not familiar with the complexities or the capabilities of the product and as such is not equipped to make a judgement on the value. You should establish control by saying, 'They can appear expensive on first inspection but what is more important at this stage is to determine which camera is appropriate for you', and the conversation is now back to establishing the buyer's needs.

You Must Control the Conversation

This will all become clearer as we go through the various stages but it is important to point out that you must dictate the flow of the conversation and you do so by sticking to the steps as described above; you see customers can very easily take over.

I remember at one time I was selling office equipment and of course I had the mandatory product brochures and very often buyers would begin by taking a brochure. They would then proceed by looking at the brochure and asking me questions. So who was controlling the conversation? They were of course. And naturally, as they were looking at the brochure they weren't listening to me and as a result my level of influence was marginal. After a few miserable commission cheques I soon learned to stick to the formula and stopped showing the brochure until it was time for me to present my case.

We, as buyers, have often seen sellers make a bags of it by not following the formula. Say you walk into a shop with the intention of buying a mobile phone. The salesperson, being a novice and not knowing the game, starts by showing you the various phones. He starts with the Nokia then the Motorola, onto Siemens and of course the little-known Korean brand. After seeing your fiftieth phone, your nodding head is getting just a little tired. Of course, not wanting to appear an idiot you decide to ask a question – big mistake. Another twenty phones are presented. Telling him you have left the kids in the car you scurry out the door. He, exasperated, walks up to his colleague and says 'What's wrong with these people? I showed him everything we had and he still walked out. Customers, a bloody nuisance!'

Of course the seller made the mistake of not following the formula; he started presenting the product before determining the need.

You see, unlike the actor the buyer doesn't know the script.

7

Finding Out What Your Customer Wants

In the last chapter I rattled on about following the structure. And what is the first thing I do – deviate from it. Is this a case of 'do as I say not as I do'? No, not at all, but I am going to start with *determining the buyer's need*. I will return to opening the sale, and, as we proceed, it will become perfectly clear, I hope.

Understanding Your Customer

As I said before, being a good talker does not mean you're a good seller. Ask yourself, what do we learn from talking? The simple answer is nothing. And learning is precisely what we need to do at these initial stages. We need to learn all sorts of things about our buyer.

We need to know:
- What are their concerns
- What are their needs
- What type are they
- What do they really want
- What money have they got
- What are their experiences

Remember everybody has views on everything. What are theirs? What is their hobbyhorse about your product or service? You will learn none of these things by you talking, only by having them talk. The more they talk, the more you learn. And learning is exactly what you need to do at this initial stage. The worst buyer you will encounter is the buyer who gives little away. I remember when I was selling key-cutting machines, mostly in rural Ireland, confronting such buyers. You know the type: arms folded and a pipe in his mouth. He'd stand glaring as I struggled on. You'd know you were under pressure as you'd feel the trickle of sweat roll down your back. And still he'd say nothing.

Selling is simple. What you do is find out what your buyer wants and then give it back to them. And it's not confined to personal selling, they all do it. Did you ever ask yourself what market research is all about?

Here we have the likes of car manufacturers running around asking idiots like you and me what shape of vehicle you like, what colour you prefer. These people who have been making cars for donkey's years spend an inordinate amount of time and money attempting to find out what you think. Surely they'd know? They've been in the car business all their lives – it's their business.

We all accept the validity of market research. It would only be a fool who would attempt to develop a product without testing the market and finding out what the buyer wants. You see, it is much simpler to find out what the buyer wants and then give it to them, than assume what they want and try to impose your views on them with the attitude of 'we know what's best'.

It is not just businesspeople who use this basic piece of common sense. Politicians also do it. They have focus groups where they gather members of the electorate and ask them what the important issues are. They then form their policies around those issues. 'What about being people of principle?' I hear you say, but that's another matter.

So in personal selling, we too apply the same common sense. We find out what the buyer wants and then we focus on those wants.

Why Customers Buy Your Product

And it is absolutely essential that we approach selling in this way. You see, buyers may buy the same product for very different reasons. The key to selling is to determine what those reasons are for your buyer. To illustrate let me ask you, what is the one thing you like about your current car? And if I asked ten car owners I could probably get ten different answers. I could get responses such as:

- Reliability
- Safety
- Resale value
- Economy
- Prestige

Yet we could be talking about the same car: same brand and same model. The point is people buy similar products for different reasons. They buy very complicated products on the basis of one or two benefits. The secret to selling is to determine what those key points are for your buyer. If the buyer's primary motivation in buying the car is reliability, then all talk of the other amazing benefits is pointless. You are talking to people about things they are not interested in – hardly the way to make sales.

Take Your Time, Understand Your Customer

Last year I took a trip to London and, like most people when visiting somewhere, I decided to go shopping. On this occasion shoes were my item of choice. When you decide to buy something it becomes a mission, so I duly made my way to New Bond Street – renowned in London for quality shoe shops. I called on a shop, very swanky indeed. I was approached by a salesperson who asked me my size and what colour I had in mind. Answers given, off he went. In two minutes he was back with three boxes in hand, nearly the height of himself. He proceeded to show me the various shoes. There was one with buckles, another with toes that were so long they looked like flippers and yet another with heels so high you would want a step to climb into them. All very fashionable but, unfortunately, none were to my taste. Off he went again and this time I'm sure I saw him scale a ladder to retrieve more boxes. Again he presented three pairs of shoes with a similar result. At this stage I looked at his shoes and immediately realised our incompatibility. The shop was like a bomb had hit it, with boxes and shoes all over the place. I made my excuses and left.

Two doors down I went into another shop. The salesperson approached, she invited me to explain what I was looking for. The chat developed and we discussed various styles. I was asked to describe my favourite pair of shoes; what I liked about them and why. After a good ten minutes and with my lifestyle and work explained, a pair of shoes was presented. Call me fussy, but I didn't like them. Before they were returned to the shelf I was asked to describe what I liked and disliked about them. This time it was not a case of scaling ladders to get more shoes but of building a ladder of agreement between me and the seller. We now had agreed what was in and what was out. The next pair were presented and of course I bought them.

Both sellers worked equally hard – if anything the first tried harder – it was just that the second seller worked *smarter* and followed the common-sense approach to selling. She started by exploring my needs, my tastes and my experience. Simple really: ask what the customer wants and then give it to them.

No One Ever Talked You into Anything

In selling there is another reason why we don't begin by talking, and it is far more subtle. Let me explain: isn't it true that no one ever sold you anything? The fact, according to you, is that you decided to buy. If I said to you, 'That's a lovely suit you're wearing, who sold you that?' you'd swiftly reply, 'The guy in the shop was a nice fella but I decided to buy it myself.' You see no one sells to you, no one talks you into anything. They might do it to others, but not to you. What happens to you is that you come to the realisation that this product or that service is right for you. You come to the realisation, but how do you arrive at that realisation?

The best way for me to explain how you come to the realisation is to give you an example. Imagine you were heading off on a week's holiday with your family. A day or so before you go, your eldest daughter points out that the camera is broken (and she'd know, she was the one who broke it). Despite the fact that you're busy trying to get organised and you have spent a fortune on this holiday already, you decide you'll head into town and pick up a camera; nothing too fancy, just a camera. You arrive into a shop and you tell the salesperson you want a camera. A mid-range camera is presented, it looks good but it's a bit pricy at €150. The sales person insists on telling you that the camera is:

- Heatproof
- Waterproof
- Produces top quality pictures

The price being a bit rich for you, you walk out of the shop. You visit a second shop and again you explain to the assistant that you wish to buy a camera; no big deal, just a camera. The assistant begins by saying, 'Before I show you our range can I ask you a few questions, so I can get an idea of what camera would best suit you?' He then proceeds to ask you a series of simple questions: 'Where do you intend using the camera?' You tell him you are heading for sunny Spain. He then says, 'I suppose you'll be around the pool most of the day?' Given it's a family holiday, you explain, the pool will be the big attraction. He asks, 'Who is going on this adventure with you?' You tell him that your wife and your three daughters (aged 18, 16 and 8) will be with you.

Next thing I see you walking out of the shop, a camera under your arm with a price tag of €275. And I say to you, 'Who sold you the camera?' As quick as a light you respond, 'No, I decided to buy a good camera. When you think about it we'll be in the sun all day hanging around the pool, you'd need a waterproof and heatproof camera. Anyway when I thought about it further, my eldest one is 18, this is probably the last time we as a family will all be away together. No, I'm happy I decided to buy a good one.'

Of course no one ever sells you anything, you decide to buy. The camera salesperson didn't sell you the camera, what he did was get you to think. To think about things you hadn't considered before, and then sell them to yourself. When you realised that this Spanish holiday was an important event for you and your family you decided to buy the more expensive camera, because it was worth the investment.

When I Thought About It, I Changed my Mind

And when you explain your decision to me you give the impression that what you bought was not what you set out to buy. And as the salesperson encouraged you to think – to consider your requirements, to think about how you would use your camera – you changed your mind.

Selling requires the seller to encourage the buyer to think and to explore issues they may not have considered before. And it happens to you all the time. You intend buying something simple and inexpensive but when salespeople explain all the implications and considerations, you buy something completely different to your original idea. And you are happy, because you have made a thorough and thoughtful decision.

This may all seem complicated but I assure you, it's not.

Telling Is Not Selling

In the first shop the seller began by telling you about the product. He explained the advantages of the camera; obviously in this case it was not persuasive and generally *telling* is not persuasive. What is persuasive is *communicat-*

ing. When the seller in the second shop began to communicate with you and asked you questions you began to think of what you required in your camera.

God Forbid

And if you don't believe me, ask anyone who has ever worked in the insurance industry what are the two most important words in that business and they'll tell you 'God forbid': 'God forbid you should be run over by a bus tomorrow and laid up for six months, but what would Mary and the kids do, how would they pay the mortgage, how would they manage and of course who'd keep up the repayments on that lovely car of yours, sure it would be repossessed?'

8

Getting Customers to Convince Themselves

You cannot talk people into anything. You can't convince them to buy a product or to accept your political view or your religious beliefs. So you shouldn't try. You'll end up annoying them and upsetting yourself.

At best, what you can do is get people to review their current thinking, to consider other possibilities and to reassess their view by thinking further on the matter. In simple language, get 'em thinking.

And as a salesperson you must decide what you would like your buyers to be thinking about. As a salesperson you will know the inbuilt competitive advantages of your product or service. And you will be anxious to have your customer thinking about issues that only your product is in a position to resolve.

Volvo, the Safe Car

For example, we all know that Volvo cars are renowned for their safety. Safety is the competitive advantage that is built into the Volvo brand. Clearly Volvo cars are also stylish, sporty and all-round good lookers.

Suppose you are a salesperson working in a Volvo dealership and in pops a potential buyer. He's a thirtysomething snappy dresser and after a few moments of conversation you get the distinct impression that your potential victim – I mean buyer – likes a little bit of flash. Now you and I know that Volvo do flash, but it's not the main offering.

You of course are mad keen to sell a car and you are well versed on the many safety features associated with your brand. You could, if you were an inexperienced seller and thought it was possible to talk people into buying, persist in telling your customer about all those wonderful safety bits and bobs. You could do the safety thing with such conviction and passion that surely even this fastidious buyer would be moved.

Moved is right – probably out the door as fast as his fashionable little patent leather shoes would carry him. As you persist in telling him about safety features, air bags, child seats and crumple zones he lost interest and you lost a customer.

However, as an experienced seller – someone who knows you can't talk people into buying – your approach is a little more sophisticated and subtle. You begin by engaging your buyer in conversation, you proceed by telling your customer that you would like to get a full understanding of his requirement and you'd like to ask him a few questions so you could get a full understanding of what he is looking for.

In the course of your discussions you ask, 'How often do you drive faster than you should?'

His response, with that knowing smile, suggests to you that we have a little boy racer in our midst. He concedes that he regularly drives too fast and, like the rest of us, it concerns him when he reflects on the potential danger.

You then ask, 'When was the last time you had a near one, a near crash?'

He launches into his most recent near-death experience. You naturally are spellbound by such daring do. Encouraged, he further explains and details how close it came to being all over. You acknowledge how frightening it can be, and even more so when you consider the carnage of an accident and what if children are involved. You both conclude that driving is indeed dangerous, frightening and full of risk.

So you say, 'Now, can I explain some of the unique advantages associated with Volvo cars...?'

So Let's Recap

At the initial stages of a sale you are interested in two things. Firstly, to establish the facts about your buyer, what their needs are, what their views are and other factual information.

Secondly, we want to communicate with our customer. By communicating I mean we need to develop a conversation. A conversation that is two-way and will encourage the customer to become aware of all the issues. You want your buyer to think, to focus on matters they may not have considered, yet when they do they will realise that your product is capable of resolving those issues and concerns.

We now know that selling is about developing conversations where we communicate and discuss issues with buyers. Telling is not selling, communicating is.

Yet most salespeople talk too much. As I have said before, sellers talk too much because they are anxious to succeed, they're enthusiastic and they are bursting to influence; and they try too hard. In selling, less is more. So you should slow down and concentrate your efforts on encouraging your customer to talk.

9

How to Get Customers Talking

We all love a buyer who spills it all out, who just gives it up. Who tells you what they want and, better still, tells you that if you can give it to them, they'll do the business.

It's great when it happens but it doesn't happen very often and that's why you, as a salesperson, are going to have to learn the skill of getting your customers talking.

How to Communicate

So how do you communicate with buyers? How do you get buyers to talk and tell you what their needs and requirements are? How do you get buyers to think about issues that should be important to them?

It's very simple really, once you start asking questions communications begin. Questions evoke a response and conversations result. Most of us, if asked a question, will respond.

If you were walking down the road and someone stopped and asked you your name my bet is you'd answer them. In fact if they progressed by asking you what county you're from, you'd probably answer that too. They're on to the third question before you ask who the quiz master is. My point is, we are primed to answer questions, if asked.

So questions evoke conversations; however, some

questions can halt a conversation while others will encourage it.

Suppose I asked you, 'Do you like sport?' There are two answers to that: 'yes' and 'no'. Alternatively, if I asked 'What sports do you like?' you will be likely to go further and explain what your sporting preferences are, if any. The difference between the questions is that one is closed while the other is open. Open questions do not result in yes or no answers and therefore by using open questions free-flowing conversations should result.

Let me give you some examples of the negative effect of closed questions. Suppose you are working in a clothes shop and a customer walks in; you approach the customer with the line, 'Can I help you?'

The customer responds with the regular reply, 'No thanks, I'm only looking.'

That's it, for you the conversation and sale are over. You can't follow the customer and say, 'Are you sure, I can tell you all about our range?' Unfortunately, it's over and simply because you used a closed question.

Other examples, say for an equipment salesperson:
Salesperson: 'Are you having any problems with the printer?'
Customer: 'No.'
Salesperson: 'Are you thinking of changing any of the equipment?'
Customer: 'No.'

Open and Closed Questions

Closed questions are conversation stoppers, so you must

avoid using them. You must use questions that involve people and encourage customers to engage in conversation.

So what are open questions and how do we use them? The most quoted explanation of open questions is provided by the English nationalist poet Rudyard Kipling:

> *I keep six honest serving men (They taught me all I knew)*
> *Their names are What and Why and When and How and*
> *Where and Who*

Most books on selling talk about open questions and describe what they are and encourage you to use them. However, it's just not that simple.

Knowing what open questions are is one thing, having the ability to use them in a selling situation is entirely different. Using open questions is something that sounds and looks easy but in practice it is difficult.

And while I'm at it, here's another complication: open questions are not natural to normal, everyday conversation. As a normal, logical person, if you want to get a direct answer you will ask a direct question. Open questions don't result in direct answers so we don't use them in normal conversation as frequently as we are required to in the selling situation.

I remember the first time I came across the idea of using open questions and was shown how they could develop conversations and get customers to talk. I was eager to use this new revelation on my next customer. Whos, whats and wheres were flying around, like condolences at a funeral.

I was so busy trying to figure out my next open question I got completely confused and hassled. Of course I had no time to listen to my customer's answers as my mind raced for the next question. All in all, it was a bloody disaster, one of those red-faced moments.

Here's a little test for you: try to have a conversation with someone about an easy subject such as sport or music and only use open questions. You'll agree it's very difficult. You are going to have learn and practise your open questions or you'll make a mess of it.

So you should use open questions but they must be planned and practised.

I will shortly outline a series of questions; you should study them and decide which are most appropriate for your product or your situation.

Questions at the Heart of Selling

Questions lie at the heart of good selling. They serve to help unearth your customers' requirements and searching questions require the buyer to think about what is important for them.

We know our questions must be open to allow for free-flowing conversations. As conversations flow the buyer is buying more than your product, they are buying you as you converse, you come closer. Have you ever been at a bar and started talking to the person next to you? As you talk you will find yourself moving physically closer and the same thing happens mentally. This is important because, as I have said before, at the start of the sale the focus is on you more than on your product. If they buy you they will buy from you.

Concentrate on Your Customer

To communicate you should ask questions but you also must listen to the answers. I'm told that we only listen about 25 per cent of the time. That's according to some research or other. Who knows who conducts all this research but I'm passing it on anyway because I thought it was interesting. When I was at school I was often told that I was only half listening. I can only imagine the reaction if I corrected the Christian Brother and informed him that 'according to research it was more likely only 25 per cent'.

Whatever the authenticity of the research, I do know that we don't listen to one another when speaking. We all know it of one another, that's why, even during conversations, we will start a sentence with 'listen till I tell you…'. What we are saying is, 'I know you are not listening to me but this bit is important, so listen.'

I don't know if listening is the correct phrase, I'm inclined to believe that it is more concentration than listening. People lose concentration and as a result don't listen. It is difficult to maintain concentration, even for professionals who depend on it. Nearly every year I'd put a tenner on Ken Doherty to win the snooker. Ken would be playing a stormer and then all of a sudden he'd miss a simple pot. The sports commentator would put it down to a 'slip in concentration'.

Salespeople lose concentration, the same as everyone else, and they stop listening. We can also be selective in our listening. Imagine you are on the bus on your way home from work. The bus is packed and everyone is talking; you can barely hear yourself think. Just then you hear two young women at the back of you talking. One says to the other, 'Then do you know what he did?' Well I'd bet more than a tenner that you'll hear the next bit.

So it is important that we concentrate on what our buyer is saying and we use our selective listening skills to our advantage. There are many obvious reasons why we should listen, not least of which is that buyers judge us and our competency on our listening abilities. Here is a classic example of this: did you ever observe people talking about medical doctors? You'll hear, 'That Dr Murphy is absolutely brutal, he hasn't a clue, someone should report him. Dr Halligan – now there's a medical genius.' Is it not amazing that people with no medical training or experience know a good doctor from a bad one? On examination you'll find that the 'good' doctors are those who listen and are attentive to their patients.

How to Influence Your Customer's Feelings Towards You

I have consistently said that your buyer must buy you before they buy from you. Now suppose I said I have an idea that will ensure that your buyers feel very positive towards you. How interested would you be in acquiring such information? Very interested I would imagine.

Let me explain by asking you two simple questions. The first is, how do you feel when you are talking to someone and they are not listening to you? The words used to describe such feelings include:

- Unimportant
- Useless
- Annoyed
- Ignored
- Upset

Now for the second question: how do feel when someone really listens to what you are saying? Such feelings include:

- Interesting
- Important

- Good
- Very positive

I know those feelings to be true and genuinely felt because I have conducted that little experiment with many groups over many years. The results are always the same. So if you want your buyer to feel good about you and important about themselves listen and concentrate on what they are saying. Listening gives you the power to influence how your buyer feels.

Wait Until You Get It All, Don't Rush

We have agreed that the start of the sale involves you asking your customer questions and listening to their answers. And when you ask questions don't be too hurried to respond to their answers by relating to your product.

If, for example, your customer is particularly interested in after-sales service, don't immediately launch into your bit on the excellence of your service. Wait, wait and wait until you have uncovered all of their requirements. You see, very often people will leave the most important piece till last.

It's a bit like when you are at home with your partner and you are having a tiff. There could be mention of squeezing of toothpaste and all that, and then of course out comes, 'Another thing, you spend too much on clothes.'

And that's it, you miserable git. You were really annoyed about the spending. It was the spending that was really getting to you; all that crap about toothpaste was only padding.

Often the last bit is the crucial bit.

The lesson is, don't rush to answer points, do conduct

a complete fact find. Even when you feel you have exhausted the investigative process, check further by summarising.

Say to the potential car buyer, 'So what you're saying is you want a car that has additional safety features with a good resale value. What else would you consider important?' Very often it is at this stage that you will unearth the nugget or the most important issue for your customer.

Sample Questions for You to Use

What we must now do is agree a series of questions that are appropriate for your product or service. I will give you a list of questions and the reasons why you might consider using them. What you must do is review these questions and possibly some of your own and enter them onto your sheet of paper. You thought I'd forgotten about that. No way, the completion of it is our expressed objective. But first, a few pointers:

1. Start with light gentle questions.
   You should start with questions that are light and not very taxing for your buyer; easy questions that can be easily answered, such as 'What prompted you to consider…?'

2. Relate to your competitive advantage.
   All products and services have inbuilt advantages. They can be very minor advantages, such as the fact that you are local or that you personally will be dealing with the customer both now and after the sale. You should ask questions that highlight the

importance of these points. Remember the Volvo salesperson who asked questions that emphasised the inevitable dangers of driving or the camera salesperson who asked questions depicting the requirement for quality.

Questions you might use:

- 'Tell me a little about your business.'
  If you are selling to businesses this is a great starter question. It is light and it allows your buyer to talk about a subject on which they are obviously very knowledgeable. You are focused on your product but you must see how your product fits into the totality of your buyer's business. You can vary this question if it is for an ordinary consumer – ask about lifestyle.

- 'How did you ever get started in this business?'
  Again, this is a good starter for business-to-business selling. Everybody has a story to tell; no doubt you have one yourself. We all enjoy explaining our amazing journey and in the telling can unveil interesting insights. I would challenge you to try this question on anyone and not get plenty of feedback. I know I have used it many times with valuable returns.

- 'How has your business changed over the years?'
  All businesses and organisations change, your buyer's perception of those changes and their challenges will give you a good insight into the type of person they are and the issues that are important

to them. You can vary the question for consumers with reference to lifestyle changes.

- 'Who else have you spoken to about this purchase?' As buyers we will often talk to a number of suppliers. Generally these competitors will have plenty to say. Asking your buyer to recall what your competitors said and what your buyer considered valuable will give you an understanding of their buying motivation. You see, the buyer will be self-selecting, they will tell you the points that were important to them.

- 'What prompted you to consider buying at this time?'
  Inevitably your buyer has a reason for considering a purchase at this moment in time. If a new carpet is under consideration maybe they want to warm up the house or they feel the existing wooden floors are too noisy. If it is a new dishwasher, maybe their existing machine was troublesome and they couldn't get parts, maybe the dishwasher was not fashionable enough. You can be certain there is a reason why your buyer is talking to you and you must explore those reasons as they will become valuable when you come to present your product.

- 'If you could design this product what components or benefits would you include?'
  The motivation for this question is clear to see. Yet it is one that is often overlooked.

The reverse of the question is also useful: 'What would you avoid?'

- 'Of other suppliers you use, which of them would you rate highly and why?'

   Very often we as sellers become too focused on our own business: our service, our products. The reality is that the inspiration for loyalty to one supplier could be transferable to your offering. If your buyer mentions customer service as a positive, it is an obvious pointer to you.

Are You the Right Man?

Clearly there are many other questions you could and should ask and which will be particular to your business.

   You should inquire as to whether the person you are talking to has the authority to buy and, if not, who else is involved. This is a lesson I learned many years ago. I drove all the way to Donegal from Dublin, about 300 miles along appalling roads, to speak to a potential buyer of a key-cutting machine. I called on the shop and I asked to speak to a Mr McGinley. The man identified himself as McGinley and I proceeded with my sale presentation.

   Without a word of a lie I spent about three hours discussing the machine and all of its advantages and how suitable it was for the business and so on. As far as I was concerned things were going great, and finally I asked for the order, whereupon Mr McGinley told me that he would tell his father all about it when he came back from holidays the following week.

What's the Budget?

You should also determine how much the customer has to spend, but don't ask them how much they would like to spend, because you are sure to be disappointed and rarely do people remain within their stated budget. In fact, such a question is a limiting factor. But it is a common mistake. What you should do is describe the range of prices and judge your buyer's reaction. Often by mentioning a premium solution you can change their expectations and leave them more open to a flexible budget.

All I have attempted to do is highlight for you the range of potential questions. You must consider what is applicable for your business and you must plan those questions and give them great thought. It is not necessary for you to ask a huge number of questions, but if salespeople have a fault, it is that they don't ask enough. They are so anxious to get talking themselves they neglect questions.

I'll let you be the judge of your current performance.

10

How to Start the Selling Conversation

Opening the Sale

Over the last week I've had three visitors to my office. Each caller was very pleasant, professional and courteous in their manner and demeanour. There was our company auditor, who came with the usual files and questions in order to complete our end of year accounts. There was a technician from the security alarm company who calls to check the system and ensure that everything is in working order. And then a salesperson came to talk to me about our printing needs for the coming year.

Of the three callers only one came with a beaming smile, thanked me for taking the time to see him and then proceeded to tell me how nice our offices were and how delighted he was to meet with me. Noticing some golf paraphernalia belonging to a work colleague of mine he began by asking me, 'How are you hitting them?'

Of course you guessed it; it was the salesperson who had the line of chat about golf, nice offices and all the rest of it. And why was the salesperson so different – so nice, so patronising and so obviously phoney?

The Barney School of Sales Training

Do you remember Barney?

I love you
You love me
We're a happy family…

I can see you getting all warm and fuzzy. Well get over it, real life is different.

The obvious, phoney and downright silly performance of some salespeople is a direct result of the silly and ridiculous training they receive. It's Barney stuff, all sweetness and light; lots of big smiles and hugs. It's for kids, not mature adults engaged in commerce and business negotiation. A lot of this stuff emanates from the States and I think it is like fine wine, it just doesn't travel. It works well in America and it fits culturally but I don't think it works this side of the Atlantic.

Let me give you some examples of this Barney stuff, and you'll know what I mean.

Smile

The smile being the shortest distance between two people, when someone smiles at you give them one of yours. So loads of big smiley salespeople, phoney or what?

Compliment Your Buyer

Notice their offices, their car, their clothes, the pictures of their kids, anything personal that will ingratiate you.
When someone comes into your workplace and starts showering you with compliments, what is your first thought: 'What's he selling?'

Be Excited

Tell your potential buyer how excited you are today to meet with them and their organisation. Yeah right.

Thank Them

Thank them for seeing you, thank them for their time, thank them for being there, thank them for being born and being born with such a pleasant face and of course tell them it has really made your day.

What utter bloody nonsense! You, like me, spotted the salesperson immediately. Yet this is the regular guff that is offered to salespeople by way of advice. If you don't believe me pick up any one of the dozens of books which line the shelves of your bookshop with titles like *How to Be the World's Best Seller*.

I don't know about you, but when someone behaves in such a fawning manner towards me, I feel embarrassed. I don't know whether I'm embarrassed for them or me, but I do know it makes me uncomfortable. I certainly know that they are being false and insincere.

So don't go around fawning over and embarrassing your potential customers. Fawning sellers are obvious sellers and as I've said so often before, an obvious salesperson is not a good one. It's about getting the balance right between being nice and sincere and being over-nice and phoney.

As for the visitors to my office I'm afraid the salesman didn't get the print order but the auditor introduced me to a payroll system that I signed up for. Who said accountants weren't sellers?

Building Rapport with Customers

If that's how you shouldn't do it, how do you approach your customer and build rapport? I suppose I could go into great detail and outline various lines for small talk. I could, but I won't for fear of insulting your intelligence. So I'll give just two pointers that have been my guiding principles.

Be Ordinary

When we are trying to impress, as we surely are when approaching buyers, there is a temptation to put on airs and graces. Our accent changes slightly or, as my mother used to say, we put on our telephone voice. It is an accent that has no geographical home and no one really speaks like it, but it's ours; well it is when we are trying to impress.

It doesn't impress so forget about it. Be yourself, be ordinary – you'll find that your buyer will be ordinary back. Most people are ordinary, that's why it's called *ordinary*. Even buyers who are a little highbrow when you meet them will resort to their ordinary state once you set the scene. You'll be more comfortable and so will they and that, in my view, is the key to building rapport.

If you don't believe me, have a look at the people you like and admire in public life. They have a shared characteristic: they are ordinary and they have the common touch. They are down-to-earth and you relate to them. Most of us tend to trust people who are like ourselves and most people are just that: ordinary.

To build rapport with your customers, be yourself.

Be Pleasant

A number of years ago I was walking through the village of Swords in north county Dublin and I met a friend of mine. We started to chat and he told me that he had recently moved into sales; he had previously worked as a technician. He was on his way to do some shopping in a small supermarket so I joined him as he walked around the shop. We were talking about everything and nothing as he shopped. Eventually we made our way to the checkout and I noticed he became quite chatty with the cashier. As we left the shop he turned and said, 'You know, I have to work at that.' 'Yes', he explained, 'I make an effort to be pleasant to people whenever I meet them, I think it helps me in sales.'

When I thought about it, it seemed like a good idea to make an effort to be pleasant. You see as we go about our daily duties it's a task to be pleasant and it does require practice.

In sales we should be pleasant – that does not mean being phoney or patronising. There's a difference and you'll know it when you see it.

For a dour technician he turned out to be a damn good salesman.

So at the start of the sale avoid all the phoney stuff, use small talk if it is what you would normally do, but, above all, be yourself and make an effort to be pleasant.

Your Opening Lines

You'll remember from the previous chapter we discussed the importance of asking questions. I said questions were the key to successful selling. I hope I made it clear that the first objective in selling was to develop the conversation, to determine your buyer's needs and to encourage your customer to think of issues they may not have thought of prior to you asking questions. All of this is achieved by you asking questions and listening to the answers.

Imagine this situation: you are sitting at your desk and you get a call from a salesperson wanting to talk to you about buying advertising in their publication. The salesperson encourages you to have a meeting so they can describe their magazine and show you how you could benefit from taking an advert in next month's edition. You agree and the stage is set.

Now ask yourself, what is your expectation? As a normal person you would expect the salesperson to meet with you and tell you of their publication. You would expect to be told of the circulation figures, the target audience, the costs and all the rest of it. However, you and I know that a salesperson should not begin by talking, but by asking questions. Now we have a problem, how do we change the buyer's expectation from being told to being asked?

Changing the Expectation from Being Told to Being Asked

The changing of the expectation is the objective of your opening remarks. Your opening lines must prepare the buyer to answer your questions. You're not a policeman with the God-given right to arrive in a person's office and start asking questions; you, as a seller, must earn that right to ask questions. And you do that with your opening lines.

For example the advertising salesperson might say: 'As I said on the phone we publish the magazine *Construction News*, which is distributed to all the major builders in the country. But before I tell you all about the publication I'd like to get an idea of your business, to see if I can be of any help to you. Do you mind if I ask you a few questions?'

You as a reasonable person will say yes and now the seller has changed your expectation and you are now poised to answer the seller's questions.

The seller proceeds with a light opening question such as, 'Tell me a little about your business?' and as you begin to talk the seller says, 'You don't mind if I take a few notes?', whereupon they open their folder and start to take notes.

So there you have it, with that simple formula the salesperson has changed your expectation and is now sitting opposite you and asking you questions and controlling the flow of the conversation by taking notes.

Other examples might include:

A salesperson in a suit shop: 'We have an extensive range of suits, and some new styles which have just arrived in, but before I show you what we have, I'd like to find out exactly what you are looking for, to see if I have something that is right for you. Do you mind if I ask you a few questions?'

A computer salesperson: 'As you know there have been huge developments in technology but before we get bogged down in all of that, I'd like to get a clear understanding of what you require from a computer and what level of sophistication you need. Do you mind if I ask you a few questions?
You don't mind if I take notes?'

A kitchen salesperson: 'Of course there are many different alternatives and any amount of domestic appliances but for me to make a recommendation I'd like to get an idea of your home and your lifestyle. Do you mind if I ask you a few questions?
You don't mind if I take notes, so I have a full picture?'

So the formula is:

1. Tell them just a little.
    Tell the buyer just a little about your product or service; explain that you have new stock or an extensive range or that you are familiar with developments in the industry. At this stage you are not putting forward your unique advantages but allowing your buyer to relax and get a sense of you.

    Confirm your interest in them. Explain that you would like to know a bit about them, to see if you can be of any assistance. Show that you are not just interested in making a sale but instead anxious to understand their requirements to see if you can help them on this occasion. This of course will build trust and will help you as the sale progresses.

2. Start with a light question.
    We have discussed in the previous chapter the type of questions you should ask. You should begin with questions that are light and easy for your buyer to answer and engage in conversation.

3. Ask if you can take notes.
    This is an important one, not only for you but for your potential buyer. Let me put it like this, just suppose you went to the doctor and after sitting for the obligatory hour and a half in the waiting room and allowing the dozen or so patients ahead of you be dealt with, your turn arrives. As you enter the consulting room you might assume that the physician sees you as just another whiner present-

ing themselves. But no, to your surprise, your doctor, forever the professional, takes copious notes as you describe your aliments.

You conclude that your doctor is genuinely interested in you and your bits and bobs.

Note-taking conveys your interest and lets your buyer know that you are serious about their requirements, as you should be. It also helps you to control the flow of the conversation.

It is as simple as that. The purpose of the opening is to ask the buyer can you ask questions. Now you might say to me, 'What if the buyer says no, you can't ask questions?' In that case you should conclude that the buyer is a moron and that you would be better off talking to someone who is a little more reasonable.

In all my years of selling I have never met anyone who has not responded in the affirmative, which is not to say that I have not met many difficult people in my selling career. As for now I'd ask you to return to your sheet of paper and write down your opening as per the formula.

11

Presenting Your Product

At this stage of the selling process you have established what your buyer wants from the product. You have asked questions, determined their needs and probably gotten an understanding of the type of person they are. You will also have build a certain amount of trust between you and the buyer. In order to bring the matter to a successful conclusion all you have to do is present your product or service. That, of course, should be very easy, seeing that you are aware of their requirements and given your knowledge of the product.

Presenting your case should be a simple process; after all it is only a matter of you talking about your product. This is a product you understand, a product you are very familiar with, a product you have talked about on a daily basis ever since you started working in this job. Well it might appear that way, but unfortunately, like most things in life, and particularly selling, it's not that simple.

But before I explain the subtleties of presenting your product to the customer, I'd like you to humour me, by engaging in a little experiment. What I want you to do is take a pen and write down three reasons why someone would buy your product or service. We'll refer to them later. I know this is another *Blue Peter* moment, but just do it.

Knowing What People Buy

I'm now going to talk about the difference between

product features and the benefits arising from those features. Those of you who have read sales books or listened to the all-familiar guru will know that they do go on about features and benefits to the point of distraction. Hopefully I won't make that mistake.

However, if you are to sell you must know what people buy, what they really buy. Of course you'd answer in a flash, 'people buy products'. But you'd be wrong. You see, people don't buy products; they buy what products do for them. They don't buy mobile phones but the ability to communicate. They don't buy torches but the ability to see in the dark. They don't buy perfume or aftershave but the allure of being more attractive to others.

Product Features, Only Half the Story

Most of us would know the facts about our product or service. We would know all the product features, all the advantages, all the bits and pieces that make our product special. However those facts and features are only half the story.

People don't buy facts and features, what they do buy are the benefits of those features. They don't buy what has been put into the product, but what they can get out of it, and this is not the same thing.

Now if people buy benefits and you are talking features I'm afraid you're not talking their language and that isn't good selling.

Let me explain all this, by a simple example. Suppose for a moment you are working in a shop selling mobile phones and you are presenting the latest phone to a teenage buyer. You could talk for a decade about all the wonderful capabilities of the handset. But ask yourself, what does this kid want from the phone? I think if you're sensible you'll realise the phone is a fashion item for this kid, above everything else this phone is about fashion. As you drone on about the satellite capabilities and all the rest of it, your buyer is wondering how cool they will look with this new adornment: 'Is this the in-phone? Does anyone else have this type of phone?'

Making the Link

Selling is making the link between what it is and what it means to your customer. The phrase to remember is, 'which means to you'. Salespeople don't simply list the features and facts about the product to their customers, they link the facts to the benefits the customer will receive.

If you ask me, that's the selling bit, making the link between product facts and customer benefits. When the seller makes the link between what the manufacturer has put into the product and what the customer can get out of it, then they are selling.

So for a salesperson selling a television, it should go something like this:

- 'It's plasma, which means to you state-of-the-art technology, so you don't have to worry about changing in a year or two.'
- 'It's flat screen, which means to you it looks well; not only a good TV, it's a nice piece of furniture; the whole room looks better.'
- 'It has teletext, which means you can get sport, news and current affairs; in fact you need never buy a newspaper again, you can save up to €10 a week on papers.'

So as a salesperson you are not listing off a series of technical facts but making a link between the features of the television and the issues that are important to your buyer: not having to upgrade, nice room, saving money.

You must ask yourself what is the customer concerned about on a day-to-day basis and then make the link, from the features of your product to their concerns and their lives.

So selling whiskey is not about ten-year-old, fine blend, Scottish Highlands, it is about relax and enjoy, drink this, and before long you'll be somebody.

As Big As Your Imagination

Since the beginning of time, people have felt a need to express themselves. When people lived in caves they expressed themselves by painting images on the walls of those caves. In recent times we are still at it.

Only a couple of weeks ago I was on holiday in Portugal and I was amazed to see that few of us can love someone, follow a football club, admire our parents or be patriotic without printing it on our bodies with irremovable ink. Tattoos are everywhere, literally. Tattoos represent yet another attempt by people to express themselves, to state who they are or how they are different.

The most common way for people to express themselves today is through products. We are what we wear, what we drive, where we live, and what and where we eat. People express themselves by their possessions; it's true and it's complex. For example a shirt with a cartoon crocodile on the breast pocket is worth a premium. A pair of trainers with a symbol that resembles a correct sign commands an exclusive price.

As sellers we must remember that buyers get more from our products than ever was put into them when they were made. If selling is about making the link between our product features and the benefits buyers hope to get from those features, the only limit is our imagination.

Now don't take my word for it. Do yourself a favour and take some time to study the adverts on television. Advertisements for cars rarely, if ever, mention technical data, but the sky is the limit in relating to your emotions. Everything from sex appeal to family values and more is offered as benefits when selling cars. As an exercise, watch a few car ads and list the benefits presented as reasons to buy. If you spot any mention of product features I'd be surprised.

It's not just car ads – it's all types of products. One of my favourites is the ad for fabric conditioner. You know the one where the little kid is getting into bed but can't get comfortable because their pyjamas are too scratchy. Yes, you, you monster, you're abusing your child because you don't use a certain brand of conditioner. Or what about the household cleaner with the pine fresh smell? There you are thinking of pine forests and mountains and they are selling you what is in effect a chemical compound. Advertisers do the same job as you: they sell products. The only difference is that, unlike you, they have about 30 seconds to make their point. They don't waste that time talking about product features, they focus on benefits, and so should you.

It's About the Customer, Not You

I hope this won't come as disturbing news, but I have to tell you that most people are like you: they're selfish. They are primarily interested in themselves. Let me put it to you this way: imagine you were invited to a family wedding and like all weddings loads of photographs are taken. The bride and groom, all the family, are in them, even poor old Aunt Margaret who, unfortunately, passed away three days after the big event.

Now the photos are ready and as you sit around the kitchen table and review the snaps who are you really interested in seeing? Is it the lovely bride or her kind and devoted husband? Is it your recently deceased Aunt Margaret, who was so loving to you as a child? Or is it you? It is, isn't it? You are only interested in looking at you. In fact you race through the photographs until you see more of you. There is the picture of the happy couple exchanging rings, and what are you interested in is, of course, the back of your head as you sit in the audience. As you ponder on that little bald spot at the top of your head you are quite oblivious and indifferent to everyone else and everything around you. You really are a selfish person, but then, so is everyone else and you need to remember that as you sell to them.

If you sell, as many people do, by saying things such as, 'We have a wide range', 'We are established since 1904', 'We have a large customer base' or 'We have four branches', it is all a case of we this, we that and we the other. Remember your customer is only interested in themselves. What you must do is take these advantages and describe to your buyer how they will benefit them. So you should say, 'We have a wide range, and what that means to you is that you can consider all the options and choose a product that is absolutely right for you.'

As a seller, what you must always do is talk about your product and its advantages as it relates to your customer, because your customer is like you, a selfish git.

Make It Crystal Clear

Before I proceed can I take a little time to tell you about the holiday I was on?

I stayed in a small hotel about 100 metres off the main thoroughfare. In the morning the sun was always shining and I would feel the heat as soon as I walked out the front door. As I made my way up the little street I'd pass a series of small cafes. Men were sitting around tables drinking tiny cups of coffee and engaged in heated conversation. They appeared to be arguing but you instinctively knew they weren't. As you passed you got that wonderful smell of coffee and you got a sense of busyness which beckoned the start of the day. As you made your way onto the main street you were greeted with tourists and the usual hustle and bustle.

Let me now ask you a question. As I described that scene, could you see it in your mind's eye? Could you smell the coffee, could you see the men? Of course you could. With that simple description, I transported you to a place in the past.

Selling is about transporting you to a place in the future. It is telling you what will happen to you if you buy this product: how you'll feel, what you'll experience. So when you are selling that car, paint the picture for your buyer: 'A new car like this offers a unique experience. Driving down the motorway with the sunroof open, U2 on the CD player, that wonderful smell of new leather…'.

You must describe how your customer will feel as a consequence of owning your product, what will happen to them, what their experience will be. Professional selling requires you to project into the future and encourage your buyer to use their imagination to experience how they will feel as a result of owning the product. You must appeal to all the senses as you describe the sensation: 'the smell of the new leather, the feel of the steering wheel and that sense of speed as you accelerate...'.

It Doesn't Come Naturally

Now if you think this will come to you as some sort of inspiration, think again. You, like all the rest of us, must work it out. You must plan it. My advice is to sit down and consider all the features of your product or service, and using the phrase *'which means to you'* list the benefits emanating from those features. Write a little storyline as to how your customer will experience those benefits as a result of acquiring the product.

Before we leave this chapter, could I ask you to review the three reasons you noted at the start as to why someone would buy your product? If you are like most people and listed product features and facts, I think it is time you got out your sheet of paper and did some work.

12

Turning Around Stalls and Objections

Once you establish the customer's needs, present your product and explain the benefits and eventually ask your customer to make a purchase they may present resistance or give an excuse for not buying. They may say:

- 'I'll think about it'
- 'I'll just take a brochure for now'
- 'It's too expensive'
- 'I don't know if I really need one'
- 'They all look the same'

Any of you who have been involved in sales will recognise these phrases only too well. All of us as buyers will have used one or all of them at some stage. It's what buyers do. And of course it is at this time that we as sellers begin to use our powers of persuasion. It is at this stage that we really begin to sell. Now we dig deep, use our influencing skills and prove ourselves as the true professionals we really are. Well, that's the theory anyway; the reality is generally a little different.

There we are all fired up, giving it our best shot and we really think we have a sale in sight, and bang out comes 'I'll think about it.' What do we do? Do we dig deep? Like hell we do. What we do is we stop selling. We say to ourselves, 'I should have known by the very look of this fella that he was never going to buy. A time waster; I should have known better.' The fact is, most of us sellers, when we get a little resistance or hesitancy from a customer, fold our tent and give up. You may, for appearance's sake, smile and give them a business card, but in your heart of hearts it's over and you want out of there. You give them the brochure and get lost.

What Do You Think?

Most selling books and experts approach this issue of handling resistance or objections of buyers by giving prepared answers to specific objections. The buyer says this, and you respond with that, and so on. For every objection you have an answer.

I think what is more important than what you say is how you feel. I think the real problem is that we ourselves begin to believe the objections. If we are constantly told that our price is too expensive we begin to believe it. If we are constantly told that our product is the same as all the rest we begin to believe it. We believe it, and we give up. We get the objection, we make a token effort and we get lost.

Let me give you an example. Suppose you put an ad in the paper for your car. This has been a great little car; unlike most things in your life it never has once given you a problem, never let you down. The most reliable and trustworthy set of wheels you ever had. And of course you are going to sell it yourself, you have that much faith in it; in fact you love it.

The ad goes in, the phone starts to ring and buyers arrange to visit. The first buyer arrives and with boundless enthusiasm you show off the car. The buyer walks around the car, looks at the clock and says, 'It has high mileage.' You greet the second buyer with some relief and again you describe your undying faith in the little beauty. More head scratching and out comes, 'Bejayus, she's been around the track.' Buyer number three makes all the right noises but eventually this tyre kicker says 'It's well worn.'

By the time buyer number five arrives you can hardly be bothered to get out of the chair. Unsmiling you approach the car, describing it as 'a high mileage, well worn, around the track type of motor.'

Can I ask you what's changed? It's the same little rocket that has served you like no other for the last two years. The type of car you would wish for a friend. Yet there you are, slagging it off.

Naturally buyers will attempt to find fault to reinforce their negotiating position. Your three-year-old son looking out the window could have told you that. You didn't sell the car but the buyers sold you with their negativity, despite your direct and definite experience of the car.

What happens is we hear something so often we begin to believe it ourselves. If you are repeatedly told something you will begin to believe it. If you are constantly told you are too tall you will eventually start to stoop as you go through doorways. Never mind that you are only five foot six. If you are told that your product is too expensive you'll buy that too.

The reason this happens is quite simple, and it's not unique to you. The fact is, you're human and human beings, by their very nature, are conformists. Just because you are a salesperson you don't stop being human and you won't stop conforming to the majority opinion. Never mind that you know buyers are presenting these arguments for their own vested and selfish interests and their assertions have no basis in fact.

How about this, let's suppose you and two friends take yourselves off to see a movie. It's billed as a thriller and it does exactly as it says on the tin. You are sitting on the edge of your seat throughout the performance. The acting is great, the plot is brilliant and, to top it all off, it's a true story. As you leave the cinema you turn to your pal on the right and you ask, 'What did you think?' and without hesitation he retorts, 'What a load of sentimental rubbish!' Your other friend pipes up with, 'Yeah, boring old crap.' Quiet as a mouse, you head home. Asked how you enjoyed the film you respond, 'It was ok, kinda boring.' You are a man of straw, you bend with the wind.

You, like the rest of us, conform to the majority opinion. You adjust your view and comply with others; you doubt your convictions in the face of dissent. In selling it's no different. If you are consistently told a negative you too will begin to doubt your own product or service. So it is not at all surprising that salespeople, when presented with objections, just make a token effort in response.

I remember myself cold calling on offices in Fitzwilliam Square – and it *was* cold calling: it was the middle of December and I was bloody freezing. I was selling office supplies, and to say things were quiet would be no understatement. Anyway I rang the bell on number 12, the buzzer went, the door opened and I was standing in this very trendy, if very green, office reception area. I gave my usual introduction and to my utter shock and surprise the receptionist said yes, she was interested in some office supplies. On this occasion the object of her desire was a desk tidy. You know the type of thing, it sits on your desk and you put your pens in it. The order value was a staggering £12. No sooner had I taken the order but I went down to the wholesaler and back in the reception area, desk tidy in hand. The company was one of those flashy graphic design places. To me that December morning it was more than that, it was a customer, one of the very few I had found in the last number of days.

I presented the product, was paid and was just exiting when disaster struck. This man descended the staircase. He had big glasses, very fashionable at the time, and had obviously come from the creative side of the business. He immediately declared that, 'No, this wouldn't work.' Absolutely not, 'the colour was wrong'. At first I thought I was overhearing an internal creative dispute over some major client account. Not wanting to miss the drama of someone else's row, I turned around. If I had known the truth I would have been gone in a flash.

The by now distraught 'creative person' had declared that the cause of the upset was the colour of the desk tidy. The shade of green was wrong. It was wrong, wrong, wrong. The now clearly embarrassed receptionist looked at me; in fact she didn't know where to look. As for me, I removed the offending item and made the long trek back to the wholesaler.

As I made my way I thought, how was I so stupid to ever think that I could sell a desk tidy without considering the importance of colour coordination; the naivety, to think that this desk tidy would not have serious implications on the corporate image of its owner. It was only by chance that this creative genius had shown me the recklessness of my ways.

Ok, I'm pulling your leg now. But the story is true and for a while I did entertain this idiot. I allowed his absurd attitude to affect me. For a time I bought his nonsense. So no matter how ridiculous the assertion of a buyer we as sellers can be influenced. If buyers tell us our products are too expensive or they are no different to any other, or in this case they are the wrong colour, we as the recipients of these comments can begin to buy the lie.

Funny enough, not long after the company went out of business. So now all their desks are tidy, ahh.

Why Sellers Don't Handle Resistance

We as sellers tend to give up when we get reluctance from buyers. Now I know you'll say we don't, but the reality is we do and we do so for all the reasons I've discussed above. I think the main reason we run from buyer resistance is that we simply don't understand buyers. We don't understand what they are doing when they are buying and what their thought processes are.

We give up because we don't understand what buyer reluctance is. So let's have a closer look at buyer behaviour. Ask yourself, when a buyer is making a purchase, what are they doing in their mind? That's right, they are making a decision. So when you are selling to people what you are doing is asking them to make decisions. Buying is called making purchasing decisions. That's it, as a seller your job is asking people to make decisions. So you should know a little about human decision making. I can tell you a couple of things:

1. People don't like making decisions.
    I know it is your job as a seller to ask people to

make decisions but the simple truth is they don't like making decisions. And it's not just big decisions; it's all sorts of ones, even little ones. Let me give you an example, say you and a friend go into a restaurant for a bite to eat. The waiter hands you the menu and you study it. After a couple of minutes you look up and say to your pal, 'What are you having?' He responds, 'I'm going for the steak.' With that you drop the menu and announce, 'I'll have the same.'

No, we don't like making decisions and we'll put decisions off and avoid them at most opportunities. You see they upset our balance and we don't like that. In fact, I believe there is a moment of madness when people go to make a decision, and I've seen it. I've been talking to a reasonable and rational person about buying a product. Next thing they go quiet, stand up, pace the floor and then in a near crescendo they announce, 'I'll do it, I'll take it.' There is obvious relief as the moment of psychosis passes.

Now I know I'm being a bit flippant, but the truth is when people are buying they are making decisions and they don't do so lightly.

2. How people make decisions.
   Let's suppose it's Friday evening, you're just finishing work and you ask a work friend, 'Are you going for a pint?' He'll probably respond, 'Where are you going to?' and 'Who else is going?' In other words, before he makes a decision to go for a drink he'll ask questions. Why? Because that's how people make decisions. They gather information

and they do so by asking questions.

When you think about it, it's only sensible that people make decisions after they gather the facts so that they can make informed decisions.

In making a purchasing decision it is no different. People make buying decisions by asking questions. However, because buying is a negotiating situation they present those questions in a negative way. So when the buyer arrives to view the car you're selling he may say, 'It looks rough, it seems to have been well used.' The real question you are being asked is, 'Will this car last, will I get further use from it?'

So let us now recap on our understanding of how people buy:

- When people are buying they are making decisions.
- When making decisions, generally they ask questions so that they can make informed decisions.
- In a buying situation those questions are often presented in a negative way.

So as a seller you should view objections for what they really are: questions. Of course they are presented in a negative manner, but know them for what they are and don't run away from them, don't just make the token effort and give up.

Let me give some examples of questions given by buyers in the form of objections:

Objection: You're more expensive.
Question: What extra am I getting for the extra cost?

Objection: Thank you but I have a supplier.
Question: What are you offering that my current supplier isn't?

Objection: They all look the same.
Question: In what way is your product different?

Objections are questions and if as a seller you see them as such you will have the will and the attitude to deal with them. In fact you will welcome objections because if you were asked them as questions you would be only too willing to give answers because you would see them as a signal that your buyer was interested.

Remember people only ask questions if they are interested. Your work friend would not bother to ask you where you were going for a drink unless he was interested in joining you; he would have just said 'Not tonight Josephine.' Questions in the decision-making process are a positive thing. So objections in the selling situation are to be welcomed, they are a sign of interest, they are a buying signal.

A Technique for Dealing with Objections

Now you should know at this stage that I'm no great fan of step-by-step solutions in selling but for the purposes of handling objections that are questions I'm going to give you a three-step technique. You should work on this one and incorporate it into your sheet of paper. I've used it over the years and with a little practice it works really well.

Step 1: Softening Statement

When you experience resistance from a buyer the tendency

is to challenge them. So your buyer says, 'Thanks, but I have a supplier.' You, being anxious to respond, may feel obliged to counter with 'Yes, but we offer a broader range...'.

Think about this, what you are doing is challenging his contention. What he must do, and will do, is defend that challenge and proceed to detail the virtues of his current supplier. In this situation you can't win.

What you must do is take the fight out of it; don't challenge but empathise with your buyer by using a softening statement. For example say, 'I understand that you are using Ark Printers and I know they do a fine job. In fact most of the people I talk to would already have a supplier.'

So the first step is to soften your response to the buyer's rebuke and acknowledge that you understand his position.

Step 2: Rephrase as a Question

Now this is the key to the technique. Take the objection and rephrase it as a question. The words you should use and you should know and learn them, are, 'I think the real question here is...'.

Let me give you some examples:
Buyer: 'I have a supplier.'
Rephrase as: 'I think the real question here is, what can we offer that your current supplier can't?'

Buyer: 'I don't need one.'
Rephrase as: 'I think the real question here is, what would be the advantage of owning a new one?'

Buyer: 'I've had trouble with your brand in the past.'

Rephrase as: 'I think the real question here is, in what way has our product changed?'

Buyer: 'You're all the same.'
Rephrase as: 'I think the real question here is, in what way are we different?'

This rephrasing takes a little practice but it is worth the effort. You must remember that it is rephrasing the objection and not just repeating it. I remember when I first learned this technique I was selling into a chemist shop in Finglas and the buyer turned to me and said, 'Thank you but I have a supplier.' Quick as lightning I said, 'I think the real question here is, you have a supplier.' He replied, 'That's not a question, that's the answer' and out the door I went. As we say in the business I got two orders that day: get out and stay out.

So take your time and learn the rephrasing technique.

Step 3: Answer the Question

This is the simple bit. All you must do now is refer to the unique advantages of your product. Explain how your product is different, what extras you are offering and the advantages that will accrue to your buyer as a result of dealing with you.

Let me put it all together in a short example. Suppose you are offering a buyer an opportunity to acquire a new mobile phone. You have presented the key benefits of the new phone and the buyer says, 'No, thanks all the same, but I'm happy with the phone I've got.' You should respond as follows:

Softening statement: 'I understand, people very often say that to me because they become comfortable with their phone and they get used to it.'

Rephrase as a question: 'I think the real question here is, will you get used to this phone and are the advantages of this handset worth you making the effort?'

Answer the question: 'It really is a simple phone, let me show you how it can make life easier…'.

People Don't Always Tell The Truth

The rephrasing as a question technique works really well when you get a genuine objection, but not all objections are genuine. You see people are complicated, they are like you and me: they tell lies.

You know how it is, suppose you are shopping for a new jacket and you go into a shop on the high street and you try on a lovely tweed jacket. You like the feel of it, you like the fit, you like the look and as you walk over to the mirror you look at the price tag, and your legs go weak. You don't turn to the salesperson and say 'Are you mad, that much for a jacket?' No, you casually take off the jacket and say, 'I'd really have to have my wife see it first.' You liar.

Now what if the seller responds with, 'No problem sir, why don't you buy it and if your wife is unhappy we'll simply exchange it?' Oh crap, but you respond with, 'Sorry, but she is away for a month and we'll drop in when she gets back.' Red-faced, you head for the door. You big, fat liar.

Do you really believe that when you are selling and the buyer turns to you and says 'That's great, but I'll have to think about it' that he is gone off to ponder?

Or how many times have buyers said to you, 'I'll give

you a call', and they don't? Do you think they lost your number? No, they are big fat liars too.

You see, most of us avoid confrontation and we'd rather tell an untruth than engage in a debate. For you as a seller this is very difficult because you can't deal with an objection if you don't get the real one. The salesperson talking to you about your wife is pointless. Now, if you had said you were concerned about the price, then the seller has a real objection he or she can deal with.

Hidden objections are a difficult issue for us as sellers. If you attempt to answer an objection which isn't the real one you will simply intimidate your buyer.

Dealing with Hidden Concerns

It is difficult to unearth people's real concerns, to find out what they are really thinking. There is only one way and that is further probing. Ask a question: 'Obviously you are unhappy about something, do you mind if I ask you what it is?'

We know certain things about people, and one thing we know is, that if you ask a person a question you will generally get an answer. People answer questions instinctively.

If you ask people to clarify something they will. Here's a simple test, ask someone to read aloud one of the rules of the road, then ask them to explain it. Most ordinary people will do just that, and respond by further explaining the rule. Logic would suggest that they would say, 'It is what it is, it's self-explanatory.' But no, they will endeavour to clarify and enlighten you. If you are with someone who is reading the newspaper with a headline that says 'Mortgage Rates to Rise' and you ask them 'What's that about?', you will find that they will answer your question and explain the headline. So we can conclude that if you ask someone a question they will answer it.

If you ask buyers what is bothering them they may tell you. So if the buyer says 'I'll think about it', you should respond with, 'It is important to take your time but obviously you are unsure of something, do you mind if I ask you what it is?' If you have a good rapport with the customer they may open up.

This is an easy-to-use and simple technique that encourages customers to explain their real feelings and concerns and allows you as the seller to deal with those concerns.

You Bring It Up

When you have been selling a product for a period of time you will soon realise that most buyers are similar and generally have similar concerns. If you sell mobile phones you will soon realise that many customers are often bedazzled by the technology or if you are selling a product that has a particular negative reputation in some respect you can reasonably expect customers to approach the buying of that product with preset ideas.

These are objections and barriers that are real and predicable. You can of course ignore the elephant in the room and wait for the buyer to mention them, but you would be well advised to consider introducing them into the selling conversation. 'What?', I can hear you say, 'Me as a seller bring up negativity as part of my selling routine? Are you mad? Customers are good enough at that themselves without me prompting them.'

There are certain advantages in you as the seller taking

the initiative and introducing concerns and questions that the buyer may have. These include:

1. If the buyer has a preconceived notion about your product they may not mention it but will filter everything you say through their preconceived ideas. An old pal of mine used to sell Fiat cars. Fiats had a bad reputation for resale values. His opening lines would always address resale. Rightly he believed that if he did not deal with this issue his buyers would harbour the concern and would not be open to his offerings. So clear the decks and deal with the concerns right from the outset.

2. If you as the seller introduce areas of concern to the selling conversation you build trust with the buyer. Trust and truthfulness are the cornerstones of good selling.

3. If you leave it to your customer to bring up the objection they then feel obliged to defend it. For example, if the Fiat car seller was to wait for the buyer to bring up the resale issue he would expect the buyer to defend the argument and then it becomes a stumbling block in the transaction.

4. As a seller when would you wish to deal with an objection – at the beginning or at the end of a sale? At the beginning of course. When you as the seller introduce the objection you determine the timing of the objection, you may introduce it at the most opportune time and prevent it from becoming a deal breaker.

By the way, my pal the Fiat salesman used to answer the resale issue by explaining that the cost was built into the price and the asking price reflected the expected reduced resale value. He would go on to say it was better to have a lower buying price than to wait for a return when you were reselling the car. I should say I have never owned a Fiat car because, while the seller's answer appears reasonable, I don't consider it convincing.

In my experience, the best way to deal with customer concerns is to anticipate them, bring them up and deal with them truthfully and honestly. Buyers are not fools but are reasonable people and will respond to reasonable explanations.

13

Getting Your Price

I'd imagine that most people are like me, that when they go out to buy something they have no fixed idea of how much they are going to spend. They have a rough idea but nothing firm. Yet when you go into the shop or when you start talking to the salesperson and are being presented with the goods your first question is, 'How much is that one, and how much is that one over there?' and so on. We are all the same, that's where we start. We start by asking the price. Buyers always mention price, they always bring it up. Even when the price is marked on the item they will ask the price: 'How much are the penny sweets?' It's normal, it's expected of them. Anyway, price is quantifiable, it's logical and we all start with it.

However, the problem is sellers become obsessed with it. They assume that because price is always mentioned it is the primary motivation in buying. They hear it so early and so often they convince themselves that the whole world revolves around price.

Let me tell you a true story to make the point. Back in the 1980s, I was running a sales training course for a group of salespeople who were involved in selling car finance. Over the couple of days we discussed a wide range of selling techniques, but inevitably the topic that kept recurring was interest rates, which for them was the same as price.

According to them the only issue of any real significance was the rate of interest – the cost of the finance. Remember it was the starving 80s and I, like most people, was up to my eyes in debt. Everything I owned was in hock, even my television was on finance. For the life of me I hadn't a clue what rate I had on any of my many loans. I began to think that I was just thick, so I enquired with a few friends as to how rate aware they were, only to find that they were just as clueless as me. In fact I discovered that my friends were just like me, they didn't give a toss about the rate, they were just glad to get passed for the loan.

Yet here I was, gathered with a group of experts in finance who were labouring under a misconception. This incestuous little group were rate (or price) mad. The reality was the only people who were really rate sensitive were themselves. The rest of us had no such obsessions, a half of a per cent here or there was of no real concern and no big deal.

Now I know that things have moved on and we are all more financially savvy, but try this little test: list your current loans and write down your current interest rates.

My point is simple, as sellers we become consumed by price, as buyers we are less driven. In truth as sellers we put too much emphasis on price and as a result it affects our selling performance. We need to have some clarity around all of this. Buyers always mention price, it doesn't mean they always buy on price. In fact, if you are selling to someone and they never ask about the price you can be sure of one of two things: 1) they are not in the market or 2) they're mad.

Buyers Don't Always Buy on Price

There is absolutely loads of evidence that buyers don't buy on price. Here's one: quartz watches are a wonderful example of technological wizardry. Irrespective of their cost, quartz watches never miss a beat. Yet not all of us wear the least expensive.

In the Dublin grocery business, which is highly competitive, Superquinn is renowned for being more expensive yet they have maintained a sizeable market share selling the same brands as their competitors.

If people bought on price then the cheapest in the market would have all of the market.

Here Is Another Thing We Know About Price

Just imagine you were buying a secondhand car and you arrived in my garage to view the range. You explain that you are interested in a two- or three-year-old small car. With that, I bring you into the showroom and I point out a little Nissan Micra, telling you it is a 2003 one-owner vehicle with a price tag of €3,400. In the corner I have another Micra, again 2003 and with one past owner; the cost of this one is €3,600.

Be honest, which car are you automatically interested in? Of course, it's the second one, the more expensive one. And you are not alone, most people would favour the more expensive car. In fact, when I described this little story to an audience one person, when asked which car would they been drawn to, shouted up, 'the better one'.

Don't be surprised, the reality is people are suspicious of cheapness. We all believe in a natural justice. If it is cheap, something has to give.

Suppose you had a terrible toothache, with unbearable throbbing pain, and I met you and told you of a pal of mine who lived just around the corner – a qualified dentist – who would pull your tooth for just €2.50. Somehow or other I don't think you'd be banging his door down.

Some years back a brand of car flooded the market. Most of us never drove one, or for that matter sat in one, yet all you had to do to get a laugh was mention its name. It was called a Lada. Do you remember the jokes?

A fella goes into a garage and says, 'Would you give me a petrol cap for a Lada?', and the garage man says, 'No deal, I won't swap.'

And what did the Lada do to deserve such merriment? It was cheap.

We know full well people do not buy on price, in fact we know people are suspicious of cheapness, yet we as sellers continually sell on price. We discount, we reduce the price, we complain that we can't get the asking price, we become obsessed with price; it becomes a self-fulfilling prophecy. What bloody nonsense.

As sellers we should not cut our price, we should sell our price. Don't give it away, sell it. As we go through this chapter I will explain how you can maintain your price and your profit margins by using simple selling techniques, but first I want to explain the true cost of a price cut or a discount.

The Real Cost of Giving a Discount

As sellers we all know how it is; you're standing there talking to a customer, you have been talking to him for the last hour, you are just about there, and God knows you need this sale. Just one more push and you'll have got him, you'll be over the line; the pressure will be off. In the salesroom, you'll be one of the boys again.

And then, without blinking, the buyer turns to you with his hand outstretched ready to shake your hand and says, 'Give me 5 per cent off and I'll write you a cheque.'

So what would you do? You'd do what I'd do, and take his hand. And I've done it many, many times. It's the natural thing to do. End the misery, get the job done, chalk it up and see another happy customer walk out the door.

It's natural, it's easy but it's wrong, very wrong, and let me explain why. But before I do, ask yourself the question: 'Would he have bought anyway?' If you had stuck to your guns and maintained your price would he have done the deal? I think you'll find that when people get to the stage of asking for a discount they have made the decision to buy, they just haven't shared it with you yet. We'll discuss this later when we are dealing with how to close the sale.

Let's have a look at the real cost of the 5 per cent discount, first in monetary or profit terms. I'm not going to get into a big arithmetic thing, but do try to follow this example.

Suppose you were selling the product at €200 with a 25 per cent profit. So you discount by 5 per cent, or €10. If you do the sums you'll find that the 5 per cent discount on the price is equal to a whopping 16 per cent cut in your profit. Look at the table below, read it and weep.

| | Cost of Discounts | | |
Selling Price	Discount	Profit	Profit Reduction
€200	0%	25%	0%
€190	5%	21%	16%
€180	10%	17%	36%
€160	20%	6%	76%

The effect of giving a discount on price has a dramatic effect on profits. A 10 per cent discount results in a profit reduction of 36 per cent. A 20 per cent discount leaves you with a profit reduction of 76 per cent. And these are gross profit figures; when you add in overheads you can see how easy it is to be a busy fool. My father would often say, 'If you work for nothing you'll never be idle.' With shortcut selling like that, you'll be very busy; never rich but busy. I know I've been that fool and it's too easy.

Unfortunately the real cost of price cutting is even worst than those figures imply and it is very often unnecessary. Let me tell you a little story I read in a book by Gavin Kennedy called *Everything is Negotiable*. I'll use my own words but here's the story.

Up in the Yukon the Eskimos would travel from place to place by dog sledge. From time to time the odd wolf would chase the sledges but the Eskimos would inevitably outrun the wolf. It was a little extra effort on behalf of the Eskimo and the dog team, but they'd make it.

Anyway this white guy is up in the Yukon. He too is travelling from camp to camp by dog sledge. One day he is out on the ice and he hears this howling, so he looks over his shoulder and sure enough a wolf is chasing him and his sledge. He shouts at the dogs and gives them a lash of the whip. As he looks over his shoulder he is convinced that the wolf is gaining on him. In a panic he wonders what to do next, and then in a moment of genius he reaches into his bag and grabs a lump of meat and throws it out. The wolf stops and eats.

The white man relaxes, but not for long. More howling and barking and as he looks back he sees the wolf again but this time with his brother; there are now two wolves chasing him. Again he grabs some meat from his bag and throws it behind him, and again he gets respite.

He hasn't gone far when there is a whole pack of wolves chasing him. Meat is been thrown by the fistful. He is down to his last morsel when he sees the camp and he barely makes it to safety.

There are a group of Eskimos sitting around a fire, and almost out of breath he tells them his story and how quick thinking he was when he thought of the meat. But far from being appreciative they were angry.

They explain that, in fact, he was not distracting the wolves with the meat, but quite the opposite: the more meat he discarded the more anxious the wolves became and the more they chased him. He was actually teaching the wolves to chase sledges.

And true to their word, from that day on the wolves chased all the sledges.

The moral of this tale is that when you give a customer a discount you can be absolutely sure that the next time you go to do a transaction with him he will demand a discount. You have taught the wolves to chase you.

What? Did you expect anything different? Did you think your customer was going to say, 'Ah you were such a nice fella last time I'll be easy on you now'? It doesn't work that way; the softer you are, the tougher they'll be.

Price Cutting Is Often Unnecessary

If you are to avoid becoming a price cutter you should learn a little about people and how they buy. Buyers ask for discounts because they know that price challenges normally work. They know that you are so keen to do the business you will probably drop your price. That doesn't mean they are buying on price, they do it because it works. They know you are a lily-livered coward and experience has shown them that price challenges result in savings, so it is worth their while having a go. They are bluffing. You should resist and hold your price, they'll buy anyway. Call their bluff.

How to Deal with Price Challenges

When a buyer asks for a discount, the first thing you should do is shock them: 'Absolutely no way, there is no way I can reduce the price.' If you do that their expectation changes and they re-evaluate. If you reply in any other way you are only encouraging further challenges. Remarks such as, 'I'll see what I can do' encourage your buyer to get tougher. Softness on your side will be rewarded with toughness on theirs.

You must respond with firmness, otherwise you are lost. You can phrase it whatever way you like but you must be steadfast. You can say, 'I have no authority', or, 'These are the written terms and conditions and I have no latitude.' Do whatever you like, but don't budge and make that very clear from the start.

I said you should shock the customer so that they re-evaluate. Let me explain how it works. Do remember when you were a child and you were about to have a scrap with another kid? This other kid was smaller and weaker than you and you were absolutely sure that you could prevail. So you square up to him, ready to do that pre-fight thing with the usual bravado and then, whack, without warning he gives you an almighty smack in the mouth. There and then, your whole world changes. You re-evaluate the situation, you reconsider, you look again at this guy and you instantly begin to search for a way out. Now all you want to do is back off.

As a seller, when you respond with a definite 'no' to a price challenge you are encouraging your buyer to reconsider and re-evaluate. Remember they were probably bluffing anyway, so you won't lose.

So that's the rule, if you get a challenge to your price, your answer is a firm NO.

Sell Your Price, Sell the Difference

I hope we are agreed that your first move should be to hold firm and hold your price. So what you don't do is drop your price; what you should do is sell your price. As we have said so many times, selling is making it easy for the buyer to buy. In this case what you should do is make it easier for your customer to accept the price by focusing on the difference, not the price.

Let me explain, just imagine you are selling an electrical appliance – say a washing machine – and your price is €655. Your customer, being a typical buyer, responds by saying that he can get the same product for €630 elsewhere.

From now on you never ever mention the full price of €655; you should now focus on the difference between your price and the lower price the buyer has quoted, which in this case is €25. After all, he has mentioned €630 so it is fair to assume that in his mind he is prepared to spend €630. The amount in dispute is €25 so never again refer to the full price.

Your job, from now on, is to deal with the difference; €25, now that's a whole lot easier than €655.

Put the Difference in Perspective

No matter whether it is €5 or €25 it is still a difference and the buyer would prefer to have it in his pocket than yours. You can't just will it away, so what you must do is put it in perspective, put it in context. Say to your buyer, 'This washing machine will last at the very least five years. So what we are talking about is €5 a year over the lifetime of the appliance.'

You are not making the difference disappear; you are putting it in context. At one time I sold office equipment and the machines were regularly €200–€300 more expensive than the competition. Generally the purchase was on lease over three years and I would point out to buyers that the difference amounted to an additional €6 per month on the lease. And when you put it that way it is a relatively small amount and it is a small obstacle to overcome. This is not a sleight of hand or a trick; it is merely saying to your customer, 'Look at the big picture and see things in context.'

It is not only salespeople who put cost in context. Regularly you will see adverts on television that use this technique. Some time ago I almost relented and bought a TV licence after seeing an ad which said that the licence fee was merely 17 cent a day. You've seen the ad: all your sport, news, current affairs and entertainment and all for 17c a day – the cost of the licence.

The ESB are also at it, if you look at the bottom of your electricity bill you will see a line which quotes the daily cost for 'all your electricity needs'.

What Extra for the Extra Cost?

Finally, to deal with the price difference you must explain

to the customer what extras you are offering for the extra cost. You should say to the washing machine customer, 'The real question here is, what extra are we offering for the extra €5 per year over the lifetime of the machine?' You then proceed to explain all the extra benefits. It can be simple things like customer service or that your location is convenient in the event of a breakdown. It need only be small things because we are talking about a relatively small amount of money.

So, to recap, the method for dealing with a price challenge is:

1. Focus on the difference.
2. Put the price difference in perspective.
3. Explain what extra you are offering.

When you focus on the difference, put the price in perspective and justify the extra cost, what you are really doing is reassuring the buyer that they are making a good decision. You are confirming that this is a fair exchange. Remember customers like to feel they are getting a fair deal. They have an assumption as to what constitutes a fair deal, and to test that they challenge the price. When you handle it as I have described your customer will be satisfied and you will be profitable; that's good business. Many of us pay a little extra for goods and services and when we can justify it we are happier and we end up as satisfied customers.

Discounting

Over the last number of pages I have argued that discounts are very often unnecessary and often counterproductive to making sales. I genuinely believe that discounting is a bad habit pursued by weak sellers. However there are times, and they are rare, when you may get involved in discounting. You should make a commercial decision as to when it is appropriate.

If you do discount, don't give it away, trade it. If your customer wants a 5 per cent discount make sure you get something in return: 'if you pay me in advance' or 'if you order two'. So for the customer who is buying the washing machine you might say, 'I'll give a discount if you can arrange your own delivery.'

The rule when discounting is simple: don't give it away, trade it. If the customer wants to change the price, you change the package. Change the package so that there is an advantage for you and you can maintain your profit margins.

Make sure your customer earns the discount, make them work for it. A deal they work for is a deal they are happy with. If you concede on a discount without getting something in return your customer will conclude that you were overpriced in the first place, that you were trying to rip them off, or worse still they will go away kicking themselves that they didn't ask for a bigger discount. And when they are talking to others about you and your business, do you think they will say 'What a nice guy, he gave me a discount'? Will they hell! What they will say is, 'That crook tried to overcharge me, just as well I'm smart enough to have pressed him hard.'

So you are a double loser: you cut your profit margin and you upset your customer. Not a good day at the office.

My advice is don't discount, sell your price and in the very rare circumstances where you must offer a discount, don't give it away, trade it.

14

Sealing the Deal, Closing the Sale

It's in every book you ever read about sales. In fact there are whole books devoted to it. Every selling course includes a section and everyone wants to learn the 'secrets of closing'. It's the ultimate trick. How can you lure the customer into making the buying decision?

There is a huge appetite for this type of stuff and there are numerous people willing to peddle a raft of techniques and tricks for closing. I know when I started in the selling business I couldn't wait to get to the bit about closing. Surely I was going to learn the ultimate secret. One based on psycho-something or other, which would turn the undecided into the happy customer. Wealth, success and a full order book was on hand.

I don't want to rain on your parade, but there is no secret to closing. There is no trick, no technique, no smart alec little ditty you can pull out at the end of a sale that will guarantee success.

Yes, there are questions that will help customers make a decision, but they are far from secrets. And we will talk about them, but as for saving the sale, I don't think so.

If there is a secret to selling, it is this. Determine what your customer wants, present your product so that the benefits match your customer's needs, answer the customer's questions and that's it, you're in business. Well some of the time anyway. There is no silver bullet and anyone who suggests otherwise is talking rubbish.

There are some very simple and common-sense truths about closing so let's start with a very obvious one: 'the more you ask the more you get'. Of course asking for the order is basic and almost insulting to spell it out in print. Yet it is amazing how many sellers don't do the obvious and ask for the business. The reason we as sellers aren't more assertive and ask the closing question is that we don't like to. It is just part of what we are, we don't like asking. It affects our sense of dignity, so we don't do it. We mistakenly think that the longer we go on, the longer we talk, the more we tell, the easier it will get. But that's not how it works. The first lesson in closing the sale is ask for the order, ask the buyer for the business. Don't wait for the buyer to give themselves up, take 'em in.

Remember the buyer knows what this is about, the relationship is well established. They know what you are: you are a seller, so stop waffling about and ask the question. You can phrase the question in many different ways but you can't avoid the question.

Not How, But When

Most students of selling are interested in how to close the sale, but what is more important than how is when. Timing is the key to closing. The right time to ask the closing question is when you get a buying signal. A buying signal is any indication from the customer that they are positive about your product. It could be an agreement about a benefit or a positive reaction to an aspect of your offering. There are an infinite number of buying signals, and you, as a well-rounded human being, will recognise a buying signal when you see or hear one. Nature has equipped you with the ability to read others, to understand body language, facial expressions and even the merest inflections.

Obviously when you get a buying signal you should ask the closing question. It's obvious but I can assure you it's not common. What most of us do when we get a positive signal is keep going. We say to ourselves, 'It's working, I'll keep going until he gives himself up.' How silly we are, when you get the buying signal you should ask the closing question:

- 'Let's get the paperwork sorted?'
- 'Would you prefer the red or the green?'

And then SHUT UP. Once you ask the question, keep your big mouth shut. Having asked, don't try to fill the void, just stop talking. Far too often salespeople can't help themselves. Trust me, now is not the time for talking. How many times have you lost the moment by asking the closing question and then followed it up with, 'Or would you like to like to see some other models?' Just shut up, as we say in selling, 'He who talks first, loses.'

So there you go, no big secret, the simple steps in closing the sale are watch and listen for buying signals, ask the closing question and then shut up.

Just One More Thing

Closing the sale is not the end, it is a beginning. It is the beginning of the relationship between you and your customer. And good selling is about winning customers, not just making sales. Loyal customers are the bedrock of a business and you start that journey once you close the sale. So you are far from finished.

For starters think about this. Suppose you go shopping one Saturday afternoon and you are buying new shoes. You walk the length and breadth of the high street. You look in shop windows, you try on shoes, you talk to salespeople and eventually you make up your mind and you buy the black shoes with the buckle. The salesperson puts the shoes in the box, walks you to the till, accepts your money and it appears as if it's all over.

But it's not, not for you. As you drive home, new shoes sitting on the seat beside you, you ponder. When you stop at the lights you open the box, you look at your new purchase. As you walk up the driveway you open the box again, another look. You're in the house, you put on the shoes, you test them out and then your partner walks in and immediately says, 'They're gorgeous; they really suit you, and I love the buckle.'

Now it's over, you have been reassured, the uncertainty since you bought the shoes has disappeared and the post-purchase blues have been dispelled.

There is a lesson for every seller in this little tale. Buyers, once they have made the buying decision, are unsure; they question whether they have made the right decision. They need to be reassured, you as a seller should begin that reassurance once the sale has been completed. Tell the customer that they made the right decision; tell them that their decision is a good one. Offer them the opportunity to exchange in the unlikely event that they should change their mind. You have started the first step in your next sale.

15

Finding New Customers Without Cold Calling

A couple of days ago I was looking around the net and I stumbled across an American site called NeverColdCallAgain.com. What a simple and great idea. It's a well-thought-out and reasoned presentation of how to avoid the most difficult and most disliked aspect of selling: cold calling.

There are only two types of people who tell you that they love cold calling. The first are thick. You would want to be really thick to enjoy such a mundane and often soul-destroying job. The others are just simple liars, who maintain this attachment to cold calling as a pretence, because it makes them look as if they are real hardcore sellers. The truth is, most of us hate and detest cold calling.

Back to our American friends who offer the 'never again' solution. I think they are similar to the fellows in the Old West who offered snake oil as the cure for every ailment. You know the type: they tell you what you want to hear and you are desperate enough to believe them. The most common version is the gang who offer diets or potions that promise to shed pounds without the unpleasant task of reducing your food intake and exercising more.

We are all suckers for this type of stuff; we'd love to believe that we can avoid the unsavoury and unpleasant and find the magic shortcut that delivers the results without the pain. I'm afraid I'm the bearer of bad news, life just isn't that simple and neither is selling.

On the other hand, there are those who insist that if you are not knocking on doors, out cold calling, you are not a real salesperson. They relish in telling you that real sellers, like real men, are those who just hit the phone and bang away. They pump you with those motivational talks that sound so reassuring that you too will eventually pipe up that you love cold calling. You of course are not that thick, you're just a liar.

The truth is that neither version is correct. It isn't that black and white – it is like most things, it's kinda grey.

Show Me the Buyers

There is no doubt that as sellers we would like to spend our time talking to people who want to buy our products. We'd like to believe that we could just devote ourselves to dealing with those who are in the market for what we are selling and we could avoid all that messing around with time wasters.

Unfortunately, selling is about dealing with all sorts of people, until you eventually meet the person who will listen to your well-seasoned argument and will be convinced that what you are offering is exactly what they want. But if you are to be a salesperson you must realise that selling involves seeking out buyers, it involves finding them and new business development is a huge part of selling.

Let me tell you a little story: many years ago I got a job selling office equipment. The office was in a basement in the heart of the business district of Dublin. The first day I arrived I was confronted with a showroom of equipment and the sales manager took me through all the machines and explained how I should demonstrate them and sell them.

I was like a sponge: I took in every word as he explained the secrets of turning potential buyers into customers. Every evening I studied the brochures, learned and perfected my presentation and assured myself that I was the guy to do the business, I knew all the benefits of all the products and how we, as suppliers, were unmatched in the equipment business.

I had a lovely folder with all the product brochures and of course an order pad, which I was sure would soon be filled with new customers who were about to be bowled over by my convincing line of chat.

Bursting with enthusiasm I eventually turned to the manager and said, 'I'm up to speed on the products and I want to get out there, and start selling. So where are all the customers I acquired?'

A little startled he turned and said, 'Follow me and I'll show you.' With that we were on our way out the door and up the stairs onto the street. He looked at me and with an expansive wave of his hand he said, 'There they are' as he looked at all the office buildings around us. He continued, 'all you have to do is find them.'

And so began the journey; what started with enthusiasm soon turned to disillusionment and eventually to panic as it dawned on me that the key to this business, as with all selling jobs, was not talking to customers but finding customers who were willing to listen. And that's the selling business: it is 90 per cent perspiration and 10 per cent presentation.

How to Find Customers

In those days and in that job it was about knocking on doors, lots of doors, until you eventually found a potential buyer. In fact I knocked on so many doors and left so many brochures that when, at last, someone was willing to listen I had almost forgotten what to say.

It was a miserable experience and, like so many other salespeople, I was sorely tempted to give it up. At times I felt like an intruder who was intent on disturbing people who were doing their work, at other times I felt I was like a beggar walking the streets. I can tell you now that if I had met someone who advocated NeverColdCallAgain.com I'd have hugged them there and then, in the middle of the street. To hell with all this macho stuff, I would have been a hugger.

Slowly and with much self-doubt I began to realise that there could be a method to this madness. I began to realise that there was a system; there was a way of doing this thing, which could work and which does work.

The Warm Knock Rather than the Cold Call

Let's be clear from the very start, I don't believe that cold calling and door knocking is the best use of a salesperson's time. I question the value of sitting down with lists and lists of random contacts and dutifully ploughing your way through them; it is not the best use of your time. In fact it is a waste of time and only serves to alienate you and destroy your motivation. It can also be bloody annoying for the people you are calling.

This is of course heresy to most in the sales business. To sprout on about marketing and how marketing should identify potential customers and provide you with leads was and is to be seen as a sissy. You were looking for an easy way out. I remember I once sold cash registers for NCR. (National Cash Registers (NCR) were the largest and best known distributer of cash machines in the world.) NCR were synonymous with cash registers but they had moved on in the technology business, they were now in higher end stuff: ATMs for banks and other more sophisticated technology. So in their wisdom they decided to hive off the cash register business. They gave an employee the agency and he ran the register business from the back of their head office on South Circular Road in Dublin. He was my boss and I was now one of his salespeople.

If ever there was a man who believed in the no-nonsense approach to selling this was him. Get out there and bang on doors. Go from one shop to another, keep going; are you a man or not? Evidently I was not, I was doing absolutely crap. To alleviate my situation I made the startling suggestion that we invest in a little marketing. I came up with the radical idea of taking a display ad in the *Golden Pages*. I had only mentioned it and I felt like a pair of frilly knickers as he stared back at me. I was gone a short time afterwards.

No way was he going to 'waste' on advertising so that wimps like me could avoid the real work – the cold calling.

Can you imagine that NCR had no advert in the most productive sales vehicle of the time, the *Golden Pages*? Here was the absolute brand leader with no ad. To even suggest one was a sign of your innate weakness.

The Warm Knock

I think cold calling is old news, it's from a different time and it has passed its sell-by date. We are in an information age with a multitude of media available to use in contacting potential customers. More importantly, we can now measure how customers interact with our message. Software allows us to do this. We have access to information that tracks buyer behaviour: it will tell you what they looked at and how long they spent, what pages they visited and where and when they exited. The extent of information and marketing intelligence is just stupendous, and it is getting better.

Google Analytics, and other email tracking software, is truly amazing. I think it is a salesperson's dream. I'm probably one of the least technical people you could ever meet but these information technology and contact management systems really rock my boat.

I have always embraced technology that helped in reducing the mind-numbing boredom of walking the streets looking for leads or phoning endless lists of the disinterested and the not in.

I naturally don't know your business but I do know that the use of information technology is the route to developing new business. Gather the lists of people who you suspect to be in the market for your product. There is any amount of suppliers of lists or you can compile data yourself but I have little doubt, the outcome of your endeavours is a product of the quality of your data. Investment in data collection and cleaning is money and time well spent.

Once you have the data it is now down to how you use it. A system I use and have used over a number of years is this: I have an extensive list of those who I believe to be potentially in the market for the product I'm selling. This list I have acquired and have developed over time. Initially I bought it and then through time I cleaned it and added to it.

You can develop lists in all manner of ways. In my case

I bought a list of human resource managers and cleaned it the old-fashioned way by phoning it. Data entry and cleaning is relatively inexpensive labour, but remember if you pay peanuts you get unmotivated and ineffective people. I have developed the data by encouraging people to join email and subscriber lists. The more innovative you are in collecting data the more successful you will be. For example, a friend of mine sells mortgages and he simply follows all the applications for planning permission. Lists are a matter of public information. Another guy I know sells to the legal profession and again lists are easily available.

Having gathered the information I simply market to it electronically using contact software. Now just in case you are technology illiterate, as I am, this is all very common stuff and easily available. The next step is to track the interaction of the list with your marketing. So if I send an offer to my subscriber list I can view how many people have interacted with the offer and I can now begin to target those people by phone. It is a salesperson's dream. You have potential buyers who have declared an interest in what you are selling.

I should add that all information is subject to the Data Protection Acts and you should familiarise yourself with the necessary legislation. The law is designed to protect people's privacy but it is not averse to legitimate marketing to those who have chosen to subscribe and have the option to unsubscribe. My advice is to check the law before you start and always respect the privacy of others.

The System for Warm Knocking

No matter how much you want it, there is no magic list of people who are going to buy from you. So like it or not, you, like the rest of us, have to engage yourself in contacting people who, at best, are *likely* to buy from you.

In selling, this activity is known as prospecting. Its name is borrowed from the gold prospectors of old, who spent their time shifting through piles of rubbish hoping to find a nugget. Welcome to the Yukon.

Prospecting is a difficult job, but it does yield to a system and that system, pure and simple, is a numbers game. And believe it or not, in prospecting for new business the biggest problem is not the response of buyers, but you and your perceptions.

Let's start with the numbers game. I know this is a hackneyed concept but over-used or not it is still true. A shop on a busy street will always sell more than one in a back lane. An advert in a newspaper with the biggest circulation will do better than one in those with fewer readers. Advertisers always quote their readership or, in the case of the internet, the number of visitors, as an encouragement to spend with them. Once you have chosen a quality list the rest is down to quantity. To use a variation of Bill Clinton's phrase, 'It's the numbers stupid!'

So how do you do the numbers; how do you make yourself a shop on the busy street? There is no doubt it's difficult, but, as I said before, the biggest problem is you.

What normally happens is you start out with great motivation and enthusiasm and you bang away. You make ten calls, nothing happens, but you're keen and you keep going. After a few more calls you begin to doubt yourself, you begin to doubt your product and your approach; all those wonderful stories and 'can do' attitude begin to fade. You decide to rethink; maybe you should look for a few tips on the internet. Recharged you go again, another belt and this time with greater zest; the voice is stronger, chin up, shoulders back; another few calls. Maybe there is another way? You think there must be a smarter way of doing this. Did you not see a site that talked about no more cold calls? Where the hell is that snake oil?

Don't Worry, You're Normal

The reason I can talk about this is because I've been there, we all have. Unless you're thick or are lying, you've been there.

What happens and what you have done is that you have made a fundamental error. You have judged yourself on the outcome of the calls. In prospecting for new business you should only judge yourself on the *quantity* of calls, not the outcome of those calls. You set yourself a target for the number of calls, you aim for that target, and you focus on that target and nothing else. If your target is twenty phone calls, that's your goal; the outcome of the call is outside of your control so forget about it. Five calls is a start, ten halfway, fifteen almost there, twenty done, you're a seller.

Ok, you sold nothing, maybe not even generated a lead. It doesn't matter; you are moving onto a busy street. If you continue to stick to your call target you will sell. I mention twenty calls as a target because it is entirely possible to make twenty calls in one hour. That's up to 120 calls a day, 600 a week, 2,400 a month. Are you getting the point? As the saying goes, the harder I try, the luckier I get.

I can tell you that I have often worked a full day with no tangible result and have gone home content with a feeling of a job well done, simply by focusing on a call target. You can content yourself by knowing that a target achieved by the day will result in sales achieved by the month.

Know Your Numbers

We all come in various shapes and sizes. Years ago, people had their clothes made for them but with the passing of time some bright spark came up with the idea that you could standardise sizes. He was right. Even the human form conforms to standards. There are standards for everything.

Many years ago I drove a van for a living. My job was to make deliveries all over the country. I would travel hundreds of miles to all sorts of locations and, of course, I was not beyond wasting a bit of time and doing the odd personal errand. I didn't get away with it: the transport manager could tell me within a fifteen-minute window how long my journeys should have taken. He was never wrong, despite all the traffic, the bumps on the road and the unforeseen he could apply a standard. No computer or information systems, just pure experience. My point is this, your business and your prospecting role will comply with a standard. One hundred calls will result in a defined number of leads and so many leads will result in a certain number of sales. If your sample is big enough you can easily work out the ratios.

There is great comfort in knowing the ratios and numbers that apply to your business. But you must know and learn the numbers that are applicable to your business; in fact it is a prerequisite for any professional seller.

A Workshop

Now I know you, like most people, are probably a little sceptical of those of us who offer formulas, like I have done, for making sales and achieving sales targets, but let me share an experience I had a number of years ago.

I was commissioned to run a workshop for a group of retail bank managers. The theme was new business development. The managers were required to sell loans and for them this was an entirely new departure. Up to that point selling loans was an alien concept; as one manager told me the norm was for customers to present themselves at the bank and enquire of the manager, 'How do I stand for a loan?', whereupon the manager replied 'You don't, you kneel like all the others.'

But times had changed, retail banking was a competitive business and the managers, God bless them, had to get out there and sell. They had to find new customers like all the rest of us and they were a little wary. And especially of someone like me who was not from a banking background.

Anyway I proceeded to explain the approach to new business as I have outlined above. The managers listened with reverence and allowed me to waffle on, nodding every now and again more out of courtesy than interest.

For two hours I explained with as much honesty and enthusiasm as I could. When I had finished I asked them for their view as to how appropriate the approach and the ideas were for their business.

As they settled back into their chairs ready to have a debate I declared that I was confident of the approach and more to the point I was ready to test it. I gave each of them a prepared list of twenty businesses in their local area and insisted that they call the list. A little shock ran around the room and more than a few objections.

I persisted and they complied, each of the ten managers returned to their hotel room equipped with their individual list. The deal was they were to take an hour calling the list attempting to generate business.

For the full hour that they were away, I walked up and down that room like an expectant father. I can honestly say that I was as nervous as a kitten. I thought to myself that I was setting myself up for a fall, a serious fall. It is one thing to advocate an approach to lead generation, it is another thing to give it over to someone else and be judged by the results. The bank was an important client for me and I was ready to get kicked.

The hour up, they returned. I asked for feedback, almost afraid to get it. As it turned out the results were great. Managers related how they had got this and that lead. They explained how they had generated various leads; in all about five real prospects had been unearthed.

With more than a little relief I finished the workshop and left knowing that my invoice would be paid.

Thinking back I needn't have worried. It was simple, think of the arithmetic: ten managers, twenty calls each, five leads.

But ask yourself what if I had spent the time talking about what you say on the phone call and regaled them with tricks for getting past the receptionist and all the other techniques that are the stock in trade of sales trainers? I'll tell you what would have happened: the managers would have hit the phones, made three or four calls and returned to the room with a tale of woo. I would have lost a client and probably a bit of dignity and they would have lost a valuable lesson.

The key to that exercise and the secret to prospecting is to have a call target. There is no doubt in my mind, and I hope yours: sales generation and new business development is a numbers game.

What about 'It'saNumbersGame.com'?

16

Sales Management

I'd like to tell you a short story about a few American guys who used to come to Ireland for a hunting holiday every year. They would stay at a small hunting lodge in Wicklow, about 50 miles from Dublin. The lodge was run by Seamus and his wife and as part of the deal he would supply his guests with guns and a hunting dog for the duration of the holiday. On the first day they were allocated a dog, a Springer Spaniel called Salesman. This dog Salesman was bred for the job and as a hunting dog he couldn't be beaten.

The Americans took off into the wilds of Wicklow with Salesman in toe. 'What a great dog' they reported when they had returned. The week over, the guests departed. For the next three years the holiday troop returned at the same time each year. They had few requirements and less demands, other than they be given Salesman as their dog. Seamus was only too happy to comply and the arrangement worked to everyone's satisfaction. The dog seemed to be the most satisfied as he grew and learned.

Then one year the hunters arrived all buoyed up and excited, ready to begin another great holiday. Same rooms, same guns and where is the faithful Salesman? With that Seamus, with a shake of his head, said 'I don't think you'll want Salesman.' Shocked, the Americans enquired further.

Seamus explained, 'Last year just after you left, an English bloke came and took Salesman out hunting. He started to call the dog Sales Manager, and ever since that day, all the dog will do is sit on his behind and bark.'

Managers

In the business I'm in I have had occasion to meet many managers at all levels. I've met some really great managers, people who have the ability to inspire and motivate others while maintaining the respect of their team; and I'd like to talk to you about how they manage and how they do their job.

Before I talk about the good ones, let me share a tale or two about the others, the bad managers. In my experience they have ranged from the bad to the mad to the plain insane. Talking about bad managers is a good starting point and it's more enjoyable.

As part of my work I very often go to companies to discuss their staff training requirements. Inevitably I would meet with the manager who outlines their requirements and gives an overview of what they feel they need. Now I know, instinctively, that we have a problem when the manager greets you with the line, 'Of course I could do this training myself, I just haven't got the time.' He, and it normally is a he, proceeds to tell you how experienced he is, how accomplished he is and tells you a few tricks of the trade. No shortage of time here, this man is on a roll. He is better than you, he knows more than you and he is going to tell you just how good he is. Oh no! I normally don't take much heed, but I can't help feeling sorry for the poor unfortunates who have to work under this man.

Let me share one of my best examples before I move on. I was given a training brief by a company and asked to prepare a proposal and present a training plan. The brief was sufficiently detailed and the contract large enough that I spent a considerable amount of time in planning and preparing my presentation. In fact I spent many hours doing research and getting an understanding of the client and their business.

I was to present my proposal to the entire sales team and they were gathered in a conference room in the company's head office. They seemed like a nice bunch of people and we got started.

I was about five minutes into my presentation when the door opened and in came the senior manager. He pulled up a chair and sat down. He sat with the group, but a little distance away. Within two minutes he was away, talking about how he saw things. Within another five minutes he was up; he walked up to me, asked for the marker and proceeded to take over the meeting. As he did so, he said to me and the group, 'They don't call me Whiteboard Maguire for nothing.' For the next hour, I and the rest of the team sat through this man's wanderings, with him playing the hero's role throughout the perform-ance. I say 'sat through'; what I really mean is 'suffered through'. By the time he was finished the audience were fit to cut their wrists. I just had to cut my losses and come to terms with the fact that old 'Whiteboard Maguire' wasn't going to listen to me, or anyone other than himself.

By the way, who would have called him 'Whiteboard'? I would say it was a DIY christening. I can only imagine what his staff would have called him when they saw the lovely Mr Maguire pulling into the car park each morning.

Pretensions

In management you can find arrogance but pretension is no stranger either. Let me give you a recent experience I had, as an example, and then we'll talk about the simple principles of good management.

Recently I received a request for a proposal for training from a software company based in Dublin. The proposal request was flowery enough but that would not be too unusual because people can often get a little stuffy when they begin to write formal business documents.

Anyway, I went to meet the three principal managers in their offices. As we say in Dublin, 'What a shower!' Here were these three self-important self-perpetuating yahoos engaging themselves in an exercise of the 'I know more convoluted management theories than you' game. And so it went on, one more pompous than the other. It reminded me of young adolescents trying to define themselves with their peers by using as many of the 'cool' words as possible.

Now I didn't get the business and you might say that coloured my perception of the three amigos; not at all, pretension is a common problem in management and organisations and it does affect the efficiency and productivity of businesses. It also engenders a culture of elitism; an attitude of sneering can pervade. Many good, sound and practical people are lost to such nonsense. I have seen it on many occasions and I would not mention it here if I didn't think it was an issue. It is an issue and it can be an important issue for young aspirants to management. My advice to young managers is to see this for what it is and stick to the basic fundamentals of common sense.

Also it is not a coincidence that the managers described

above were cut from the same cloth. What happens is a senior manager is infected with this pretentious gene, and they actively recruit others like themselves who in turn become carriers. Before you know it, you have an organisation that is flawed throughout.

How It Goes Wrong

I shouldn't be slagging managers I've met because more often than not it isn't their fault. A lot has to do with how managers are recruited and trained. What normally happens is a management position becomes available and the best salesperson becomes the newest manager. It is not just sales, it happens in every area of management. And very often it doesn't work because being good at a job does not equate to being a good manager. They are different jobs with different skill sets. What can happen is that the business loses their best seller and gains a bad manager. It is unfair to the new appointee because they are in a job they are not capable of doing, the business suffers because the best salesperson is gone and the sales team suffer because they are now managed by someone who hasn't a bloody clue. Sound familiar? It should, it happens all the time.

The results of such a mistake go as follows: the new manager in his naivety or innocence believes the management job requires him to catch people doing it wrong and correct them. And so it goes, he keeps trying to catch them doing it wrong, and they just get better…at not being caught.

Another Way

If the sales manager was properly trained he would know that the key to good management is not about catching people doing it wrong, but catching them doing it right. Catch them doing it right, recognise them for doing a good job, acknowledge their achievements and reward them with praise. If people are acknowledged and recognised for their achievements they tend to repeat the performance. Therein lies the key to management: recognition.

If you can get your head around the power of recognition you are on your way to being a good manager.

The essence of good management is catching them doing it right. But to do that, you and your team must know what constitutes doing it right. If you were simplistic, which you are not, you would say getting it right for the salesperson is hitting sales targets and doing the numbers. You measure salespeople by their sales – wrong, very wrong.

Sales Measures

Sales figures are often the only measure for salespeople and it can be hugely damaging. Did you ever have the experience of a bad month, just everything going south and the more you try the worse it gets? The most difficult time to sell is when you are not selling.

So now after your lousy month you have to go to the monthly sales meeting. The first thing the manager puts up on the screen are the sales figures. And you sit there squirming, you have gone into the meeting sore and you are now bleeding. This public admonishment just adds to your humiliation: 'So Sean, you are having a bad month', says the manager. As if you didn't know, as if you haven't been under stress for weeks, worrying about the damn figures.

Something is wrong about this. At a time when you are

most vulnerable, you are most down, your manager leads off by giving you a good kicking. Surely this is wrong, what you need is support and encouragement. Your manager should be offering help, advice and guidance. He should be asking the team to give you a boost to get back on track, not inviting them to give you a boot now that you are down. But that is what happens time and again at sales meetings.

Don't Judge Salespeople on Sales

Let's be clear about one thing, salespeople have no control over sales. They have control over their effort to produce sales. They have control over the number of calls they make, the quality of their presentations, the time they devote to new business development, the number of contacts they have in their database and so on.

To manage salespeople and to drive their performance you should set clear guidelines and standards for all selling activity. You should legislate for how you expect them to perform. If you manage the inputs you are guaranteed the outcomes. If you prescribe how someone should do their sales job you can predict outcomes, you can predict sales.

Now I can hear you say, 'That's micro-management, it's a bit over the top.' Nonsense, I'll tell you what is unfair – it is unfair not to offer salespeople the day-to-day guidelines and specifications to deliver sales and then to bully them when they fall below target. To fail to give salespeople standards is to fail them.

If you as a sales manager still use sales results as the only measure of performance you are not doing your job. It is a case of 'show me the baby; don't tell me about the labour pains'.

Standards of Performance

The headings listed below are typical areas where we should set standards of performance.

Business Development Activity

- Number of calls per day
- New business calls
- Customer service calls
- Additions to database per week
- Email shots to database

Presentations

- Defined structure of call
- Opening
- Fact-finding
- Benefits of product
- Dealing with objections
- Closing techniques

Personal Image

- Appearance
- Style guide for written communications
- Templates for proposals

Administration

- Service level agreements
- Completion of documentation
- 'Must haves' when on a sales call
- Recording of activities and action plans

Clearly I can't give the definitive list for your particular situation and job but you get the idea. The message is more management not less, more direction not less, more engagement with inputs so that you can influence outputs. By the way, salespeople prefer specifics as to what is expected of them. It takes the guesswork out of their job.

Conclusion

When I was a kid, like most other kids, I believed in myths and fairy tales. And there were a lot of them about. There was all that Hansel and Gretel, Little Red Riding Hood stuff. Mind you, I got over that very quickly, and like other kids in my class we would listen to the teacher with that 'yeah right' look on our face. We were young but we weren't thick. Granny dressed as a wolf? Give me a break.

There were other fairytales that were more enduring and more debilitating and were not confined to junior infants classes, but were to be part and parcel of the fabric of society. One classic was that work was for ordinary people and business was for business people. Now the teacher didn't sit at the top of the class and announce that this was the case. No, we just concluded that that was the way it was. Ordinary people did ordinary jobs and business people did business jobs; business jobs, where you wore a suit, and went to an office. We assumed that such well-dressed, well-groomed and often well-spoken folk were smarter than us. They worked on a different level, they were better than us and they knew things that were very complicated. They weren't and they aren't; it was a myth, a fairytale. Business is not complicated and it is not complex. I have spent my entire adult life working in business and the one lesson I have learned above all others is that business is basic. The good and brilliant business people I have met and worked with over many years are those who know and do the basics. Business and a career in business are within the grasp of anyone of ordinary ability.

Another fairytale is the one about sales people. The one that suggests that selling and those who have 'mastered the art of selling' are somehow different to the rest of us. Sellers have hidden psychological powers, demonic motivation and of course all the tricks, techniques and insights to turn the most sceptical of buyers into adoring and loyal customers. Sellers are different, they are confident, articulate and pleasant looking. They could sell snow to the Eskimos – of course it's a fairytale. It's a fairytale on a scale that makes Hansel and Gretel look like a documentary.

At the beginning of this book I told you that selling is simple, straightforward and basic common sense. Yes, there are a few rules and I hope as you read through the pages you concluded that they make sense and there is logic and reasoning to them. I hope you also concluded that selling is for everyone and anyone. Anyone who applies the simple basic logic can become not only a good seller but an expert seller, capable of competing at any level. Obviously, the mere knowing of the principles of no-nonsense selling will not guarantee you success. You have to mix that with the other ingredient mentioned in this book, simply titled 'hard work'.

The thoughts and ideas outlined in this book are a direct result of my experience. The lessons I learned as a young fella in the cut and thrust of the direct selling business are all here. They have served me well and provided a very good living.

The greatest school of all is the school of experience, but the fees can be very expensive.

Planned Sales Presentation

Your Opening Lines

_____
_____
_____
_____
_____

Questions

_____
_____
_____
_____
_____

Unique Selling Benefits

_____
_____
_____
_____
_____

Possible Customer Concerns

_____
_____
_____
_____
_____

Closing Statements

_____

_____

_____

_____

_____

_____